—Ripe
Recipes
A Third Helping

Beatnik

This book is dedicated to the customers, team and suppliers who have supported Ripe over the past 15 years.

First published in 2018 by Beatnik Publishing

Text: copyright © Angela Redfern & AMR Consulting 2018

Photography: copyright © Sally Greer 2018

Illustrations: Amy Melchior

Design, Typesetting & Cover Design: copyright © Beatnik 2018
Designers: Sally Greer with special thanks to Akin who developed the new brand for Ripe Deli
Artworkers: Martin Berweger, LeeAnne Berney & Lucy Sykes-Thompson

Ripe Creative Director: Amy Melchior

Recipe Development, Food Styling & Testing: Amy Melchior with help from
Andrea Saunders and the talented team of chefs and bakers at Ripe Deli

Printed and bound in China

ISBN 978-0-9941383-4-7

Beatnik

PO Box 8276, Symonds Street
Auckland 1150, New Zealand

www.beatnikpublishing.com

—Ripe Recipes
A Third Helping

ANGELA REDFERN

Beatnik

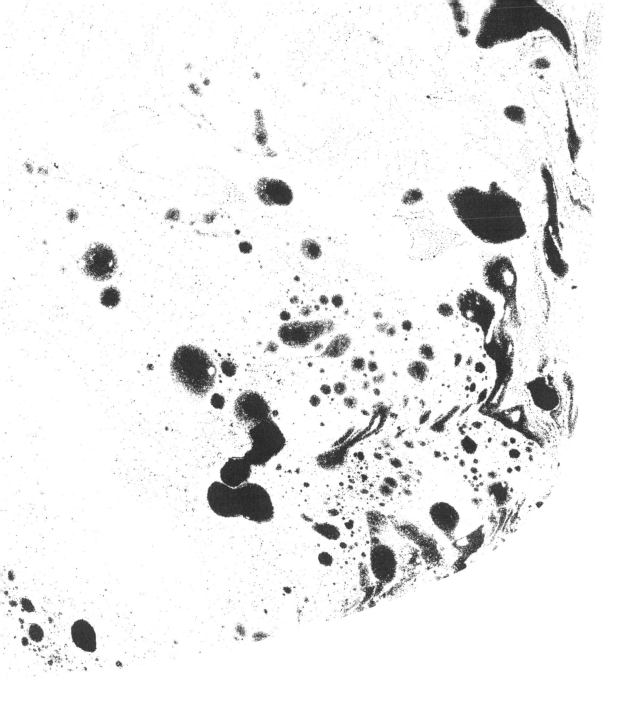

One of the very nicest
things about life is the
way we must regularly
stop whatever it is we
are doing and devote
our attention to eating.

— *Luciano Pavarotti*

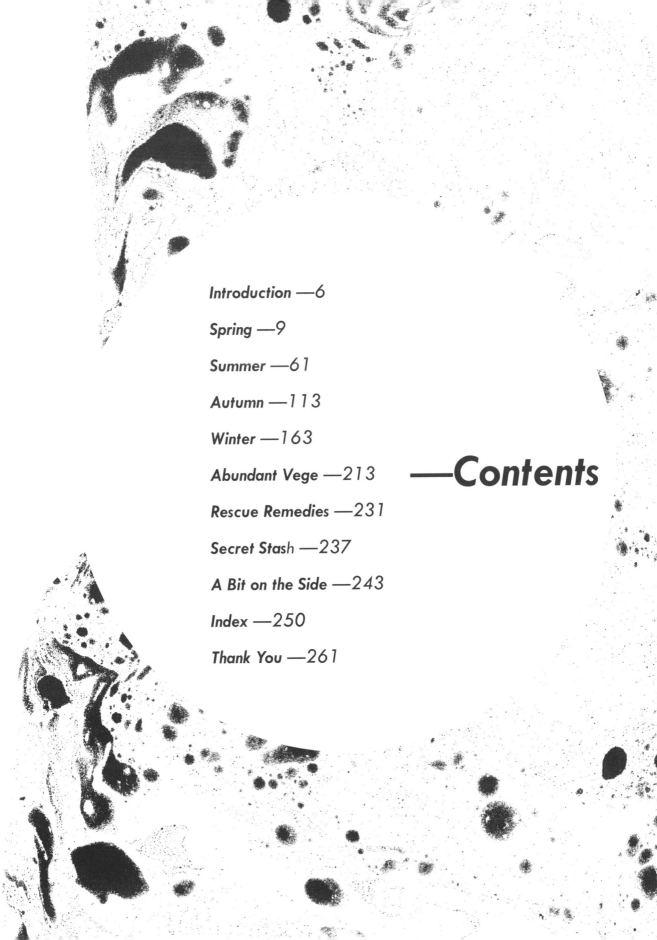

—Contents

—A Third Helping

On a sunny day in December, we popped a few bottles of the bubbly stuff at Ripe and raised our glasses to our team and customers – after all, without them there would have been no reason to celebrate. The milestone? 15 years since we opened the doors of Ripe Deli in Grey Lynn for business. And boy what a decade and a half it has been.

We've literally watched our customers grow and evolve. In fact, there are now people on our team who I remember as being gorgeous-faced toddlers, holding hands with mum as they waddled in for their fluffy and marshmallow.

It's been fascinating to be involved in all the food trends that have come and gone in that time. When we first started, vegan food was a rarity and now it's a fundamental part of our business. The only choice of milk

you had was green or blue. Now there's a full-flung milk menu, including coconut and fresh almond. Apparently there are hemp, pea, flax and quinoa milks on the horizon – watch this space!

In 15 years we've seen kale and quinoa explode onto the food scene. Pasta went from being a constant number 1 hit to being almost shunned (thankfully it's recovered!), replaced by the quiet infiltration of grains, which crept in and established themselves in most of the dishes we offer. We navigated the fresh juice craze... and then retired our big old juicer when slow pressed juices and kombucha came in and took centre stage. If you told me 15 years ago that we'd be using 'chicken-free chicken' I would have laughed at you but, what do you know, we're currently trialing recipes using it...

From paleo politics, to dairy-free dishes and gluten-free goodies, to hardly cooking at all with the raw food movement, we've seen a lot change over the past 15 years – and our knowledge of different foods has developed and grown with all of it.

We're an open-minded bunch at Ripe – we love trying new things, getting creative in the kitchen and continuing to evolve, especially when it results in beaming smiles from our customers. But despite all the changes, some things have stayed the same.

Our food is – and always has been – wholesome. We like to use what's in season and create dishes that make your taste buds sing. We like to make food that is good for the soul – and if that means a little slice of ginger crunch at times, so be it! We believe you should eat what you desire but eat conscientiously, enjoy it and be grateful for it. Our efforts to be sustainable in all facets of the business have never waned.

Ripe has always been unashamedly local. We love our customers and we love the community we live in. We've wholeheartedly supported local schools, businesses, charities and events. We get a buzz from community spirit and love to give back, whether that's through free meals, vouchers or the proceeds of selling worm wee. We are very much sharers – of our time, our products and our recipes...Which brings me to this book.

A third cookbook wasn't even on my radar last year. It was our busiest yet: we opened one new store and were head-down planning a third one; we undertook a re-brand for Ripe, the first since opening; and

then there was the matter of two small humans keeping me very busy at home! But how could I say no to our amazing creative director Amy Melchior when she broached the idea about sharing more recipes with the world?

A Third Helping is filled with our last 5 years of food evolution. As always, putting it together was a bit like a shared lunch: we asked people (the past and present Ripe Deli team, friends, some suppliers) to contribute their best recipes – things they love making and seeing others eat. I also put in a few specific requests for things I wanted a good recipe for, like the Beef Phó (on pg 36) and loaded it up with great salads, as that is what we are most known for.

As a result, A Third Helping is filled with customer favourites, recipes

we're famous for, and recipes our staff wish we were famous for!

As well as getting creative in the kitchen, we got a bit creative in the design too. Michelle Ineson, the wonderful illustrator from our previous books, had headed overseas to start a new adventure so Amy Melchior (being a practicing artist as well as a chef) jumped on board to illustrate the book. Amy used everything from garlic, mushrooms, lemongrass, kale and even fish to create the prints you'll see throughout. Food is literally art in this cookbook.

A Third Helping is dedicated to the customers, team and suppliers who have supported us over the past 15 years. From the bottom of our hearts, we thank you.

Angie Redfern

Budding flowers

Snow peas and snowdrops

Longer days

Newborn lambs

Daffodils

Fresh new growth

Sweet scented blossoms

—Spring

Banana, Maple, Coconut Muffins

Makes 12

DF, VEGAN

Light and moist vegan muffins with salted coconut caramel glaze – oh so good! We recommend doubling the recipe for the caramel so you have some handy to drizzle over your favourite fruit for pudding.

MUFFINS

1⅔ cup (250g) **SELF RAISING FLOUR**
⅓ cup (50g) **COCONUT SUGAR**
¾ cup (75g) **DESICCATED COCONUT** + extra for garnish
½ cup (125ml) **MAPLE SYRUP**
150ml **COCONUT CREAM**
50ml **WATER**
½ cup (125ml) **VEGETABLE OIL** or melted **COCONUT OIL**
1 tsp **VANILLA EXTRACT**
½ tsp **SALT**
1 cup **MASHED BANANA** (aprox 3 bananas)
1 **BANANA** thinly sliced on an angle – for garnish

SALTED COCONUT CARAMEL

6 tbsp **COCONUT SUGAR**
¼ cup (65ml) **WATER**
1 cup (250ml) **COCONUT CREAM**, we recommend Kara
1 tsp **VANILLA EXTRACT**
A pinch of **FLAKY SEA SALT**

Preheat oven to 180°C.

Grease and line a standard 12-cup muffin tin with paper muffin cases.

To prepare the muffins: in a large mixing bowl combine all the dry ingredients together. Add the maple syrup, coconut cream, water, oil, vanilla, salt and mashed banana. Mix until well combined.

Spoon the mixture evenly into lined muffin cups. Top each muffin with some sliced banana and a sprinkle of coconut. Bake for 25 – 30 minutes or until a skewer inserted into the centre comes out clean.

To prepare the salted coconut caramel: in a heavy based saucepan, mix the coconut sugar with the water. Place over a medium heat and cook for a minute or so until the sugar has dissolved into the water.

Bring to a simmer and add the coconut cream while stirring constantly – be careful, it can splatter a bit.

Simmer for 10 – 15 minutes or until the caramel starts to thicken. Remove from the heat and stir through the vanilla and salt.

To serve: drizzle some of the salted coconut caramel over the top of the muffins and serve the rest on the side with coconut yoghurt.

Dreamy Creamy Goat's Cheese Tart

Serves 12

VEGETARIAN

This is the perfect tart for a sunny spring picnic at the park, amongst the blossoms with a chilled glass of wine. You can, of course, use savoury shortcrust pastry instead of the savoury oat crust if you wish.

SAVOURY OAT CRUST

2½ cups (250g) **QUICK COOK ROLLED OATS**
1 cup (150g) **WHOLEMEAL FLOUR**
2 tbsp **FRESH ROSEMARY**, finely chopped
1 tsp **FENNEL SEEDS**
1½ tsp **SALT**
200g **BUTTER**, melted
1 **EGG**

FILLING

120g **CREAMY FRENCH GOAT'S CHEESE**
250g **RICOTTA**
¾ cup (180ml) **CREAM**
3 **EGGS**, separated
2 cloves **GARLIC**, peeled, very finely chopped
2 **SPRING ONIONS**, white and green parts, finely chopped
1 cup (40g) **MIXED FRESH HERBS** – we used **BASIL**, **PARSLEY** and **CHIVES**, finely chopped
½ tsp **SALT** and freshly **GROUND BLACK PEPPER**
ZEST of 1 **LEMON** + 1 tbsp **FRESH LEMON JUICE**

TO SERVE

3 cups (120g) **ROCKET** or **SALAD LEAVES**
¼ cup (10g) **MIXED FRESH HERBS – BASIL**, **PARSLEY** and **CHIVES**, roughly chopped
1 tbsp good quality **BALSAMIC VINEGAR**
1 tbsp good quality **EXTRA VIRGIN OLIVE OIL**

Preheat oven to 180°C.

Grease a 30cm fluted tart tin.

To prepare the oat crust: using a food processor, blend all the ingredients for the crust until well combined.

Firmly press the oat mixture into the base of the prepared tart tin, pushing some of the mixture up the sides to create an even crust. Using a fork, prick the base a few times. Place in the freezer to chill for 10 minutes.

Once chilled, place in the oven to bake for 10 – 15 minutes or until lightly browned. Remove from the oven and set aside to cool a little.

To prepare the tart filling: in a mixing bowl, whisk together the goat's cheese, ricotta, cream and egg yolks. Add the garlic, spring onions, fresh herbs, salt, pepper, lemon zest and juice. Mix until well combined.

In another bowl and using a whisk or handheld electric beater, whip the egg whites until soft peaks form. Fold the whipped egg whites through the cheese mixture until well combined.

Pour the mixture into the tart shell and bake for 20 – 30 minutes or until the egg custard is just set. Remove from the oven and allow to cool for at least 10 minutes before removing it from the tin.

To serve: place the tart on a large platter and slice into 12 pieces. Top with the rocket or salad leaves and herbs. Drizzle the olive oil and balsamic vinegar over the leaves.

Japanese Okonomiyaki Prawn Pancake

Serves 4 to 6

GF, DF

These savoury pancakes are really tasty and will become a firm favourite. This is a gluten free version, but plain flour works as well. You can also add grated carrot or shredded greens to this mix, just swap it cup for cup with the cabbage. For a vegetarian version, use tofu instead of prawns.

PRAWN PANCAKE

4 cups (400g) **GREEN CABBAGE**, (approx ½ a large cabbage) *finely shredded*
3 **SPRING ONIONS**, *white and green parts, finely chopped*
1 tbsp **PICKLED PINK GINGER**, *finely chopped*
¼ cup (10g) **FRESH CORIANDER**, *finely chopped*
1 tbsp **SESAME SEEDS**
1 cup **PRAWN MEAT**, *finely chopped*
¾ cup (150g) **GLUTEN FREE FLOUR**
¾ cup (180ml) **WATER**
3 **EGGS**
1 tsp **SEA SALT** *and freshly* **GROUND BLACK PEPPER**
1 – 2 tsp **SRIRACHA** *or* **SAMBAL OELEK**
2 tsp **GLUTEN FREE SOY SAUCE**
2 tsp **SESAME OIL**
SESAME OIL *and* **VEGETABLE OIL** *for frying*

FOR THE TOPPING

OKONOMIYAKI SAUCE (see pg 244) or **TERIYAKI MARINADE** (see pg 235)
JAPANESE MAYO (see pg 245)

To prepare the pancake batter: in a large mixing bowl place the shredded cabbage, spring onions, pickled ginger, coriander, sesame seeds and prawn meat. Mix until well combined.

In another bowl whisk together the gluten free flour, water, eggs, salt, pepper, sriracha or sambal oelek, soy sauce and sesame oil.

Pour the wet mixture over the cabbage and prawn mixture and toss to coat the cabbage and prawn mixture in the batter. Set aside for 10 minutes to allow the batter to rest.

Place a large frying pan over a medium to high heat. Add a dash of each of the oils. Place a large heaped spoonful of the mixture into the frying pan. Spread the cabbage out so the pancakes are about 1cm thick.

Cook the pancakes a few at a time, allowing space for them to spread.

Tip: keep mixing the batter through the cabbage each time you cook a pancake to ensure the cabbage is well coated in batter.

Fry each pancake for a few minutes on each side until crispy and cooked through. Set aside to drain on paper towels. Repeat this process until all of the pancakes are cooked.

To serve: drizzle the pancakes with Japanese mayo and okonomiyaki sauce or teriyaki sauce. These pancakes are best eaten as soon as you have cooked them so they are nice and crispy.

Note: these pancakes are delicious served with Japanese mayo and either okonomiyaki sauce or teriyaki sauce, all of which you can find in most supermarkets or your local Asian supermarket. We have included gluten free recipes for all of these sauces in this book as most store bought varieties contain gluten.

The Sisters' Marinated Red Lentil Salad

Serves 4 to 6

DF, GF, VEGAN

A wonderful salad created by two amazing sisters Tina Brown and Shana Pito. I am forever grateful for the many hours of hard work these ladies put into Ripe. They created so many delicious and creative dishes at Ripe over the years; we miss their laughter and kindness. It's been great to see them go forth and start up their own catering company.

SALAD

½ cup (100g) **DRIED SPLIT RED LENTILS**, soaked overnight – see note below
¼ cup (60ml) **FRESH LEMON JUICE**
1 **APPLE**, core removed, thinly sliced
1 **AVOCADO**, de-stoned, diced
1 head **BROCCOLI**, cut into bite sized pieces
1 packet (180g) **CRUNCHY BEAN SPROUT MIX**
½ punnet (50g) **ALFALFA SPROUTS**
¼ cup (10g) **FRESH MINT LEAVES**, leaves picked and torn
¼ cup (10g) **FRESH CORIANDER LEAVES**, roughly chopped
¼ cup (10g) **FRESH ITALIAN PARSLEY**, roughly chopped
2 cups (180g) **SILVERBEET**, **KALE** or **SPINACH**, finely chopped

MAPLE LIME DRESSING

½ cup (125ml) **FRESH LIME** or **LEMON JUICE**
½ cup (125ml) **OLIVE OIL**
2 tbsp **MAPLE SYRUP**
A pinch of **SALT**

To prepare the lentils: place the lentils in a large bowl and cover with plenty of cold water. Stir through the lemon juice and leave to soak overnight (this helps to break down the phytic acid in the lentils; you can leave them even longer and sprout them if you have the time).

After the lentils have been soaked, rinse them very well under running water for a few minutes, until the water runs completely clear. Drain well.

To prepare the dressing: in a mixing bowl, combine the lime or lemon juice, olive oil, maple syrup and salt. Add the apple, avocado and lentils to the dressing and mix well. Set aside to allow the lentils to marinate for at least 20 minutes (the longer the better).

To serve: place all the remaining ingredients for the salad into a large serving bowl. Add the apple, avocado, lentils and all of the dressing. Mix well to combine.

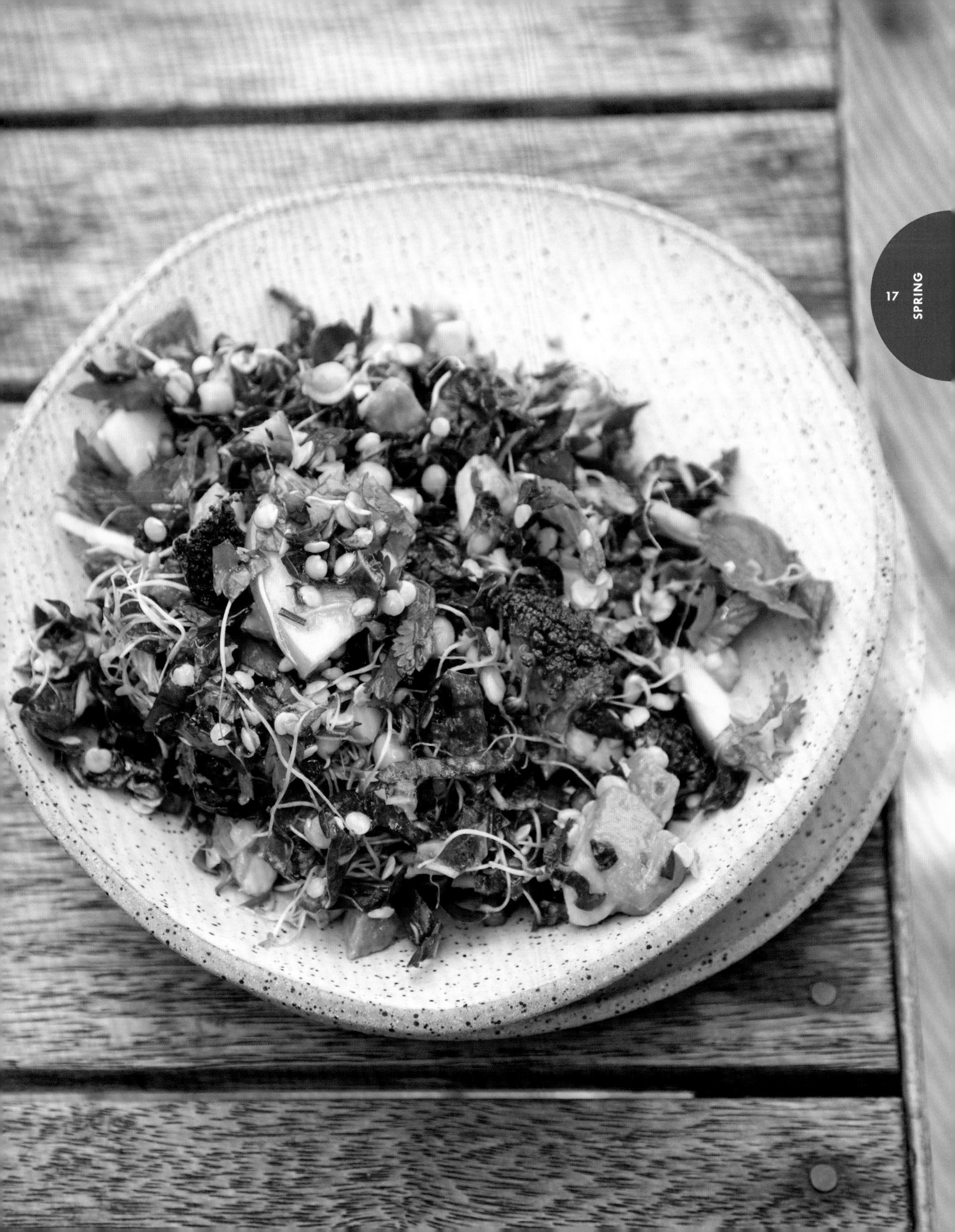

Anwar's Slaw

w/

Spicy Sriracha Mayo
+ Sticky Barbeque Chicken

Serves 6 to 8

DF, GF

Anwar Geor, one of our great chefs, created this taste sensation. It is a perfect slaw bursting with flavour. Serve with warmed wraps as an easy meal. This is a large recipe but it is easily halved.

SLAW

½ cup (125ml) **ASIAN STICKY BARBEQUE MARINADE** (see pg 235)
  or **TERIYAKI MARINADE** (see pg 235)
2 **CHICKEN BREASTS**, thinly sliced into strips
2 tbsp **SESAME SEEDS**
2 tbsp **VEGETABLE OIL**
½ (300g) **RED CABBAGE**, finely sliced
2 cups (200g) **MUNG BEAN SPROUTS**
1 **CAPSICUM**, stem removed, de-seeded and thinly sliced
2 cups (80g) **BABY SPINACH**
½ cup (20g) **FRESH CORIANDER**, roughly chopped
2 **SPRING ONIONS**, white and green parts, finely chopped

SPICY SRIRACHA MAYO

1 cup (250ml) good quality **MAYONNAISE**
3 tbsp **SWEET CHILLI SAUCE**
3 tbsp **SRIRACHA CHILLI SAUCE**
¼ cup (60ml) **FRESH LIME JUICE**
¼ tsp **SALT**

In a small bowl, mix the Asian sticky barbeque marinade or teriyaki marinade, sliced chicken and sesame seeds together. Set aside to marinate for 10 minutes.

Place a large frying pan or wok over a medium heat and add the oil. When hot add the marinated chicken. Stir-fry for 3 – 5 minutes until caramelised and cooked through. Remove from the heat and set aside to cool.

To prepare the mayo: mix all the ingredients together in a small bowl.

To serve: in a large serving bowl, combine all the vegetables for the slaw. Add the chicken and toss well to combine. Season to taste.

Drizzle over half of the sriracha mayo and serve the remaining mayo on the side.

Raw Chop Chop Salad

w/

Avocado, Broccoli + Almonds

Serves 4 to 6

DF, GF, VEGAN

This salad is all about the dressing. We love avocado; anything smothered in this creamy herby avocado dressing is going to make your taste buds sing.

AVOCADO DRESSING

¼ cup (10g) **FRESH BASIL** or **FRESH CORIANDER**, *finely chopped*
¼ cup (10g) **FRESH ITALIAN PARSLEY**, *finely chopped*
1 clove **GARLIC**, *peeled, crushed and finely chopped*
¼ cup (60ml) **AVOCADO OIL** or **OLIVE OIL**
½ ripe **AVOCADO**, *skin and stone removed, roughly chopped*
¼ cup (60ml) **FRESH LEMON JUICE**
3 tbsp **CIDER VINEGAR**
1 tbsp **MAPLE SYRUP** or **HONEY**
½ tsp **SALT**

CHOP CHOP SALAD

1 head **BROCCOLI**, *finely chopped*
¼ (300g) **GREEN CABBAGE**, *chopped into bite sized pieces*
½ **CUCUMBER**, *diced*
1 **CAPSICUM**, *stem removed, de-seeded and diced*
½ cup (20g) **FRESH CORIANDER**, *stem and leaves finely chopped*
½ cup (20g) **FRESH ITALIAN PARSLEY**, *roughly chopped*
200g **GREEN BEANS**, *topped and tailed, finely chopped*
1½ ripe **AVOCADOS**, *peeled and stone removed, cut into bite sized pieces*
¼ cup (30g) **NATURAL ALMONDS**, *toasted and roughly chopped*

To prepare the dressing: place all the ingredients into a bowl. Using a stick blender, blend until the dressing is smooth and green.

To serve: place all the vegetables into a large serving bowl. Add the dressing and toss the vegetables to coat them well. Sprinkle over the almonds and serve.

Oh Baby Baby!

—

Black Quinoa, Baby Potato + Asparagus

w/

Hot Smoked Salmon

Serves 6 to 8

GF

All the good stuff mixed into one fabulous hot salad! Creamy new baby potatoes and feta, sweet asparagus, hot smoked salmon, the goodness of quinoa, smothered in a zingy caper dressing.

SALAD

600g **BABY POTATOES** *cut any big ones in half*
½ cup (100g) **BLACK** *or* **RED QUINOA**
2 bunches (approx. 500g) thin **ASPARAGUS**, *woody end trimmed, chopped in half*
2 cups (400g) **EDAMAME BEANS**, *shelled*
½ cup (20g) **FRESH ITALIAN PARSLEY**, *roughly chopped*
½ **RED ONION**, *peeled, finely diced*
2 tbsp **CAPERS**
200g **HOT SMOKED SALMON**
200g **CREAMY FETA**, *crumbled*

CAPER DRESSING

3 tbsp **CAPERS**
2 tbsp **FRESH LEMON JUICE**
½ tsp **SALT**
½ cup (20g) **FRESH ITALIAN PARSLEY**, *roughly chopped*
1 – 2 tbsp **HONEY** *or* **MAPLE SYRUP**
2 tbsp **CIDER VINEGAR**
¼ cup (60ml) **OLIVE OIL**

To prepare the potatoes and quinoa: in a large saucepan place the potatoes and quinoa. Fill with enough water to cover the potatoes. Place over a high heat and bring to the boil.

Cook for 15 – 20 minutes, until the potatoes are cooked through. Remove from the heat and drain through a sieve. Set aside in the sieve to cool a little.

To prepare the asparagus and edamame: using the same saucepan, refill it with hot water and place over a high heat. When boiling, add the asparagus and edamame beans. Cook for a couple of minutes, then drain and refresh under cold running water.

To prepare the dressing: place all the ingredients into a small bowl. Using a stick blender, blend until well combined and the dressing turns green.

To serve: in a large serving bowl, place the potatoes, quinoa, asparagus, edamame beans, parsley, red onion and capers. Pour over the dressing, add half the feta and toss to combine. Flake over the salmon and top with the remaining feta.

Get Your Freekeh On

—

Broad Bean + Pea Salad

Serves 4 to 6

DF, VEGETARIAN, VEGAN OPTION

Freekeh is a lovely whole-wheat grain that is roasted and smoked in the fields and then sun dried. It is used a lot in Middle Eastern dishes. You will find it in health food shops or Middle Eastern food stores, although if you cannot find it you can use coarse cracked Bulgur wheat instead. For a vegan version substitute the honey for maple syrup.

SALAD

1 cup (160g) **FREEKEH**

3 cups (500g) **BROAD BEANS**, *fresh or frozen, shelled*

1 cup (110g) **PEAS**, *fresh or frozen*

½ **RED ONION**, *peeled, sliced into rings*

½ **TELEGRAPH CUCUMBER**, *diced*

1 ripe **AVOCADO**, *de-stoned, peeled and diced*

½ cup (20g) **FRESH ITALIAN PARSLEY**, *roughly chopped*

¼ cup (10g) **FRESH OREGANO**, *leaves picked*

¼ cup (10g) **FRESH MINT**, *leaves picked and torn*

MINT DRESSING

3 tbsp **WHITE WINE VINEGAR**

2 tbsp **FRESH LEMON JUICE**

2 tsp **DIJON MUSTARD**

¼ cup (60ml) **OLIVE OIL**

2 tbsp **HONEY** (or **MAPLE SYRUP**)

¼ tsp **SALT** and freshly **GROUND BLACK PEPPER**

1 tbsp **FRESH OREGANO**, *finely chopped*

2 tbsp **FRESH MINT**, *finely chopped*

To prepare the freekeh: place the freekeh in a saucepan with 3½ cups of water. Place over a medium heat, cover with a lid and bring to the boil. Cook for 15 – 20 minutes, until the grains are tender. Drain and set aside to cool a little.

To prepare the broad beans and peas: place another saucepan filled with water over a high heat and bring to the boil.

When boiling add the broad beans and cook for a few minutes (fresh broad beans will take a little longer to cook than frozen ones), then add the peas and cook for a minute or so longer. Drain and refresh under cold running water. Remove the skins from the broad beans.

To prepare the dressing: place all the ingredients into a small bowl and using a stick blender, blend until well combined.

To serve: in a large serving bowl, place the freekeh, broad beans and peas. Add all the remaining ingredients for the salad. Pour the dressing over the salad and toss to combine. Season to taste.

Andrea's Herby Pasta Salad

w/

Asparagus + Tuna

Serves 6 to 8

The fabulous Andrea Saunders created this lovely salad full of the green goodness of spring. It's a large and plentiful salad that is a meal in its own right.

PASTA SALAD

500g good quality **PASTA**
OLIVE OIL – for drizzling and frying
2 x 300g bunches **ASPARAGUS**, woody ends trimmed, cut in half
1 cup (130g) **FRESH** or **FROZEN PEAS**
1x 65g jar **CAPERS**, drained
120g **HALLOUMI**, thinly sliced
1 x 185g can **TUNA**, drained
ZEST of 1 **LEMON**
¾ cup (100g) **GREEN OLIVES**
½ tsp **SALT** and freshly **GROUND BLACK PEPPER**
2 **SPRING ONIONS**, white and green parts, finely sliced
3 cups (120g) **ROCKET**
1 tsp **SALT**

HERBY VERDE DRESSING

1 cup (40g) **FRESH BASIL LEAVES**
1 cup (40g) **FRESH CURLY PARSLEY**
1 cup (40g) **ROCKET**
1 tbsp **FRESH MINT**
1 tbsp **FRESH ROSEMARY**
1 clove **GARLIC**, peeled, crushed
1 tbsp **CIDER VINEGAR**
1 tbsp **HONEY**
½ cup (125ml) **OLIVE OIL**
JUICE of 1 **LEMON** (aprox ¼ cup)

To prepare the pasta: cook the pasta following the instructions on the packet. Place the cooked pasta in a large serving bowl, drizzle with a little olive oil and toss to coat the pasta in oil.

To blanch the asparagus and peas: fill a large saucepan ¾ full of hot water and add a pinch of salt, place over a high heat and bring to the boil. When boiling, add the asparagus and cook for 1 – 2 minutes or until just cooked through.

Using tongs remove the asparagus from the boiling water and place in a colander; refresh under cold running water. Add the peas to the boiling water – if using fresh peas cook for 1 – 2 minutes or until tender, for frozen peas cook for just a minute. Drain and refresh under cold running water.

To prepare the capers: using a couple of paper towels, squeeze all the liquid you can out of the capers. Place a frying pan over a high heat with a splash of olive oil. When hot add the capers and fry for a few minutes until nice and crispy. Remove from the heat and place on paper towels to drain.

To prepare the halloumi: place the pan back over a high heat, add a good splash of oil and when hot add the halloumi. Fry until golden on both sides. Remove from the heat and place on paper towels to drain.

To prepare the herby verde dressing: using a food processor or stick blender, blend all the ingredients together until well combined, smooth and bright green.

To prepare the salad: pour the dressing over the pasta and mix well. Add the asparagus, peas, tuna, lemon zest, green olives, salt and pepper to the pasta and toss to combine. Adjust seasoning to taste. Gently mix through the spring onions and rocket. Scatter the crispy capers over the top and serve.

Italian Marinated Vegetable Salad

Serves 6

DF, GF, VEGAN OPTION

Quick, easy, crunchy and delicious – what more could you want? You can eat this salad straight away but try and plan to have leftovers as the flavours of this salad just keep improving the longer it marinates. For a vegan version substitute the honey for maple syrup.

SALAD

300g **BROCCOLI**, cut into small bite sized pieces
300g **CAULIFLOWER**, cut into small bite sized pieces
2 **CELERY STEMS** + some of the tender leaves, thinly sliced
½ **RED ONION**, peeled, thinly sliced
1 **CAPSICUM**, de-seeded, stem removed, diced into small bite sized pieces
1 cup (40g) **FRESH ITALIAN PARSLEY**, roughly chopped
½ cup (100g) **MARINATED ARTICHOKES**, roughly chopped
½ cup (100g) good quality **MIXED MARINATED OLIVES**
2 tbsp **CAPERS**
¼ cup (10g) **CHIVES**, finely chopped

MARINADE

¼ cup (60ml) **SHERRY VINEGAR** or **CIDER VINEGAR**
3 tbsp **FRESH LEMON JUICE**
2 tbsp **HONEY** (or **MAPLE SYRUP**)
¼ cup (60ml) **EXTRA VIRGIN OLIVE OIL**
1 tbsp **WHOLEGRAIN** or **DIJON MUSTARD**
¼ tsp **SALT**

In a large serving bowl mix all the vegetables and herbs together.

To prepare the marinade: in a small bowl mix the vinegar, lemon juice and honey (or maple syrup) together until well combined, then whisk in the olive oil, mustard and salt.

Pour the marinade over the vegetables and herbs then toss well to combine. You can serve this salad straight away, but it is best left to marinate for at least 20 minutes in the refrigerator.

This salad's flavour will keep developing over time and it keeps well in the refrigerator for at least a few days.

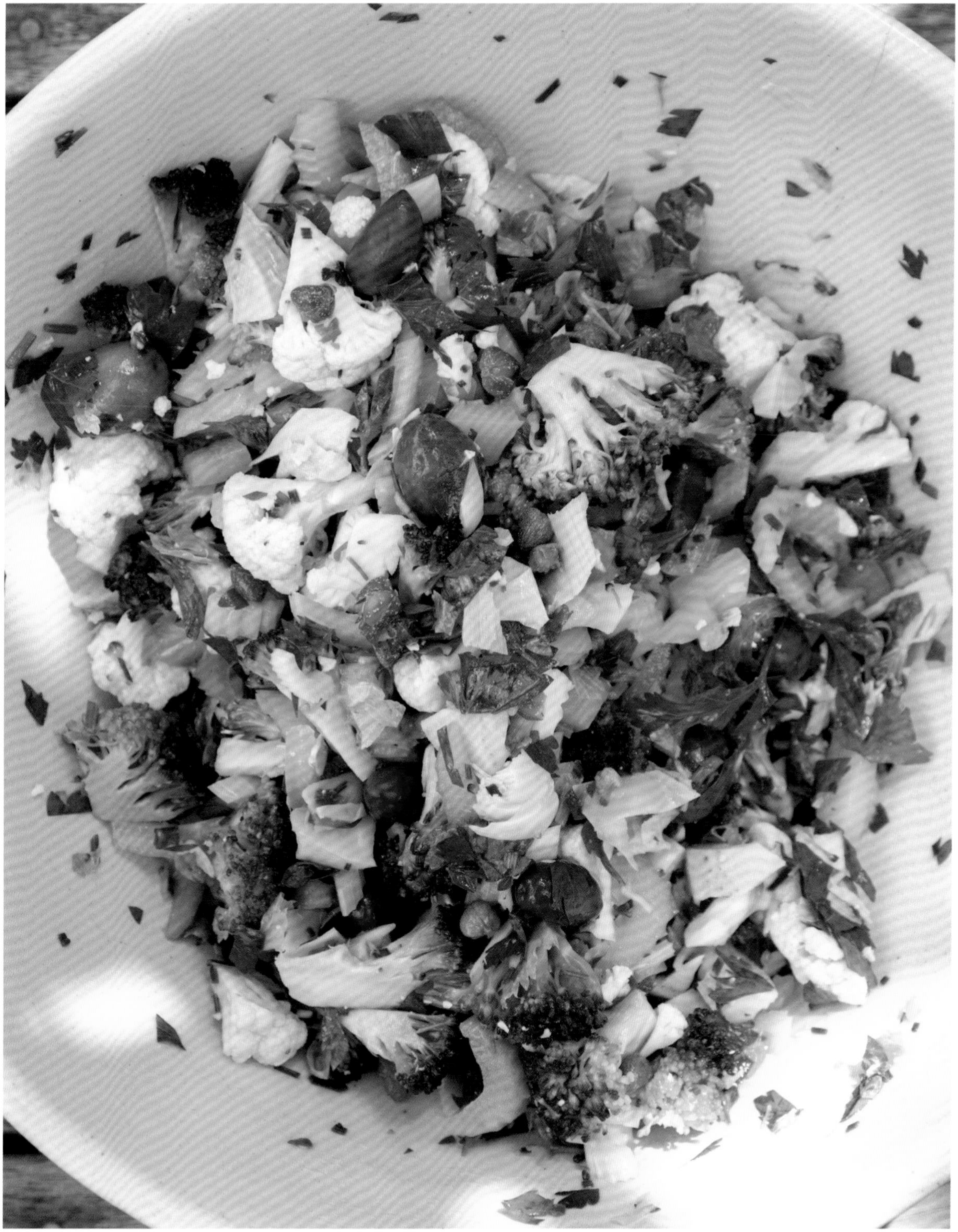

Maggie's Spanakopita

Serves 10 to 12

Maggie McMillan is a great addition to the Ripe team; she has created many wonderful new dishes for our cabinets. There is something very comforting about spanakopita. Layers of crispy, buttery filo, with creamy salty cheeses and fresh greens – it's a heavenly pie. Thanks Maggie for this lovely recipe. We use spinach in this recipe but any dark leafy greens like cavolo nero, silverbeet or kale taste great too.

SPANAKOPITA

2 tbsp **OLIVE OIL**

2 **ONIONS**, peeled, finely sliced

3 cloves **GARLIC**, peeled, finely chopped

½ tsp **SALT** and freshly **GROUND BLACK PEPPER**

200g **FETA**, crumbled

250g **RICOTTA**

50g **PARMESAN**, freshly grated

7 **EGGS**, lightly beaten

400g **SPINACH LEAVES**, roughly chopped

1 cup (40g) **FRESH BASIL**, roughly chopped

1 cup (40g) **FRESH ITALIAN PARSLEY**, roughly chopped

120g **BUTTER**, melted

1 x 375g packet **FILO PASTRY**

Preheat oven to 180°C.

Grease a 30cm fluted tart tin with melted butter.

Place a frying pan over a medium heat and add the oil. When the oil is hot, add the onions and cook for a few minutes or until the onions are translucent. Add the garlic, salt and pepper and cook for a few seconds until fragrant.

Remove from the heat and transfer the mixture to a mixing bowl. Set aside to cool slightly. Add the feta, ricotta, Parmesan and eggs. Whisk the mixture together until all the cheeses are well combined with the eggs. Stir through the spinach and fresh herbs.

To assemble the pie: lightly butter 4 sheets of filo and place them one on top of the other in a stack. Repeat this process 4 times, so that you end up with 5 stacks of buttered filo sheets.

Place 4 of the stacks of filo into the tart tin, overlapping them so the base and sides are well covered with the filo.

Note: leave some of the filo hanging over the sides of the pie tin.

Pour the filling into the tin. Lightly scrunch up the last sheets of buttered filo and place it on top of the pie. Fold the overhanging edges into the middle of the pie. Brush the top liberally with butter.

Place the pie on the lowest shelf in the oven and bake for 40 – 50 minutes or until the filling is set.

Note: if the filo is browning too quickly, loosely cover the top of the pie with foil. Once the pie is cooked leave it in the tin to cool for at least 10 minutes before cutting.

Helen's Black Beans

Serves 4 to 6

DF, GF, VEGAN

Altezano Brothers have been supplying Ripe with amazing coffee since the very beginning. This is their late mother Helen's frijoles negros recipe, from their childhood growing up in Central America. "Our family clocked up many miles on the road, and a favourite ditty of ours was, 'beans, beans, the musical fruit, the more you eat, the more you toot, the more you toot, the better you feel, so eat some beans at every meal!'"

BLACK BEANS

500g **DRIED BLACK BEANS**, soaked in plenty of water for a least 4 hours or overnight

THE SLOW COOKED BEANS

3 tbsp **OLIVE OIL**

1 **RED ONION**, diced

4 cloves **GARLIC**, peeled, crushed and roughly chopped

1½ tbsp **GROUND CUMIN**

1½ tbsp **SMOKED PAPRIKA**

1 tbsp **DRIED OREGANO** or 2 tbsp **FRESH OREGANO**

2 tsp **WHOLE BLACK PEPPERCORNS** (or freshly **GROUND BLACK PEPPER**)

2 x 400g cans **DICED TOMATOES** or 10 large **RIPE TOMATOES**, diced

1 tbsp **TOMATO PASTE**

1 tsp **SALT**

1 lt **VEGETABLE STOCK** or **WATER**

3 – 4 **CHIPOTLE CHILLIES** in **ADOBO SAUCE** (optional if you like it hot), finely chopped

1 cup (40g) **FRESH CORIANDER**, roughly chopped

THE POT BEANS

3 tbsp **OLIVE OIL**

2 **ONIONS**, peeled, diced

6 cloves **GARLIC**, peeled, finely chopped

1 tsp **SALT**

Note: this recipe is cooked in two parts – the "Pot Beans" and the "Slow Cooked Beans" which are then combined to make a delicious black bean casserole.

To prepare the beans for cooking: once the black beans have been soaked, remove any beans that have floated to the top. Drain well and rinse very well. Divide the soaked beans into two even portions.

To prepare the slow cooked beans: preheat oven to 180°C.

Place a flameproof casserole dish over a medium heat and add the olive oil, onion and garlic. Cook for a few minutes until the onion is translucent. Stir through the cumin, smoked paprika, oregano and peppercorns. Cook for a few seconds until the spices are aromatic.

Add the canned or fresh tomato, tomato paste, salt and stock or water and add one portion of the beans. Stir through the chipotle chillies (if using). Increase the heat to high and bring to the boil, then cover the casserole dish with a tight fitting lid and place in the oven to cook for 2 hours, or until the beans are very soft.

To prepare the pot beans: place the other portion of the beans in a large stockpot. Add just enough water to cover the beans. Place over a high heat and bring to the boil. Once boiling, reduce the heat to a gentle simmer for 1 hour or until the beans are very soft.

Note: you will need to top up the water every now and then while the beans are cooking.

Remove the "Pot Beans" from the heat and blend with a stick blender or food processor. The beans should be slightly runnier than hummus. You may need to add some water to get the right consistency.

Place a large frying pan over a medium heat. Add the oil, onions, garlic and salt and fry for a few minutes, until translucent. Stir the pureed "Pot Beans" through the onion mix and cook for a few minutes.

To serve: once the "Slow Cooked Beans" are cooked, add the pureed "Pot Beans" into the casserole dish and mix well. Adjust seasoning to taste and top with the fresh coriander.

Serve with warmed corn tortillas or natural blue corn chips. Side dishes of salsa (or salsa verde), guacamole or fried halloumi are all delicious additions. For a good kick of heat, serve with hot chipotle chilli sauce. Try adding spicy csabai or chorizo sausage to the casserole for a meaty option.

Beef Phó Broth

Makes approximately
8 — 10lt of broth

GF, DF

To make a really good phó broth you need a big stockpot and some time up your sleeves – though for at least 6 hours of the cooking time you can walk away and do other things. I think it's worth the wait as the result is a very delicious nutritious broth that is great for your gut and general wellbeing.

I recommend freezing some of the broth so you have some handy for future use. We use beef leg bones, including the knuckles – you will find them at your local butcher. Ask your butcher to saw them into small pieces for you so they fit in the stockpot. We also use oxtail as it gives a lovely meaty flavour to the broth.

BROTH

2kg **BEEF BONES**, *cut into 10cm pieces*

1 kg **OXTAIL**

2 **ONIONS**, *root left on, halved and peeled*

1 whole **BULB GARLIC**, *leave the bulb whole, thinly slice the base of the bulb off*

1 large piece **FRESH GINGER** *(approx. 10cm), skin on, sliced in half lengthways*

15 whole **STAR ANISE**

1½ whole **CINNAMON STICKS**, *broken into small pieces*

15 whole **CLOVES**

2 tbsp **FENNEL SEEDS**

3 tbsp **CORIANDER SEEDS**

1 x 20cm piece of **MUSLIN CLOTH** *and a length of* **NATURAL FIBRE STRING**

2 **BAY LEAVES**

2 tbsp **PALM SUGAR** *or* **COCONUT SUGAR**

1 cup (250ml) **FISH SAUCE**

2 tsp **SALT**

To prepare the bones: using a very large stockpot (with at least 15lt capacity), add all the bones and fill with just enough water to cover them. Place over a high heat and bring to a rapid boil.

Cook for approximately 5 minutes or until a bubbly scum from the bones forms on the surface of the water — don't cook them too long or you will lose all the good marrow from the bones. Drain and discard the water, rinse the bones and rinse out the stockpot.

To prepare the onion, garlic, ginger: you need to char the onions, garlic and ginger. You can do this over a gas flame using metal tongs, turning them until they are well charred. Alternatively use the grill in your oven. Set it to its highest grill setting, place them onto a baking tray and place under the grill to char. Make sure you turn them so they are evenly charred on all sides.

To prepare the spices: place a frying pan over a medium heat and toast all the spices until fragrant. This should only take a minute or so, the cinnamon stick may take a little longer.

When they are cool enough to handle place the charred onions, garlic and ginger, along with all the toasted spices, on the piece of muslin cloth and tie it tightly with the string to make a small secure bundle.

To cook the broth: place the parboiled bones back into the clean stockpot. Add the bundle of onions, garlic, ginger and spices to the stockpot along with the bay leaves and sugar.

Fill the pot ¾ full of water and place over a medium heat. Bring to a simmer. As soon as the pot starts to simmer move it to the smallest element on your stovetop and reduce the heat to as low as it can go.

Leave broth to cook for 6 hours very gently and without too much movement — so don't stir it. Every now and then skim off and discard any oil, foam or scum that forms on the surface with a large spoon.

After 6 hours remove the bones and the bundle of onions, garlic and spices. Strain the broth through a sieve. You can pick off any meat left on the oxtail bones and add it back to the broth, if you like, or use it in another dish. Stir through the fish sauce and salt.

You can ether serve some of the broth straight away, by following the recipe for Beef Phó, or pour some into large jars to keep in the refrigerator and freeze the rest.

Beef Phó

Serves 6 to 8

GF, DF

Phó is all about the aromatic flavours of the fresh herbs mixed with the silky lightly spiced broth. Phó is a fun meal to share with family and friends as it's very interactive, which is especially great for kids, as everyone gets to decide what they would like in their bowl.

The beef is served raw but when the hot broth hits the beef it cooks immediately, which is always exciting to watch. We prefer to use eye fillet for this dish as it's a lovely tender cut of meat, but sirloin or round eye will work as long as it is trimmed well and very thinly sliced.

PHÓ

3 – 4 lt **BEEF PHÓ BROTH**
2 whole **STAR ANISE**
500g **BEEF EYE FILLET** or **SIRLOIN**, trimmed of any fat and sinew
1 x 250g thin dried **RICE NOODLES**
3 cups (300g) **WHITE CABBAGE**, finely sliced
120g **MUNG BEAN SPROUTS**
3 **SPRING ONIONS**, white and green part finely sliced
3 cups (120g) **FRESH HERBS – THAI BASIL, MINT** and **CORIANDER**, roughly chopped
2 **FRESH LIMES**, cut into wedges
2 – 3 **FRESH CHILLIES**, seeds removed if you don't like it hot, finely chopped
3 tbsp **WHITE VINEGAR**
2 tsp **COCONUT SUGAR**
SRIRACHA CHILLI SAUCE
HOISIN SAUCE and/or **SOY SAUCE**

To heat the broth: pour the broth into a large saucepan and add the star anise. Place over a medium heat and bring to the boil. When boiling reduce the heat and keep at a gentle simmer until you are ready to serve. Taste the broth to check the flavour. If it is a little strong you can add some hot water at this point or you may want to add a splash more fish sauce to boost the flavour a bit.

To prepare the beef: place the beef on a chopping board and slice into very thin slices. **Tip:** if you freeze the beef first this makes it easier to slice thinly, or you can use a mandolin to slice the frozen beef. Place the sliced beef in a serving bowl and set aside.

To prepare the noodles: place the rice noodles into a bowl and cover with warm water to allow them to soften for 5 minutes before you cook them. Place a large saucepan ¾ full of hot water over a high heat and bring to the boil. When boiling, add the soaked noodles (drained) and cook for a minute or until just cooked through. Drain and refresh under cold running water, place into a serving bowl and cover with warm water – this will stop them from sticking together.

To serve: place the cabbage, mung beans, spring onions, herbs and lime wedges in individual piles onto a serving platter. Place the chillies into a small bowl, add the vinegar and sugar and stir until the sugar is dissolved. Place the bowl of chillies and the bowl of cooked rice noodles on the table along with the bowl of sliced raw beef. Serve with sriracha chill sauce, hoisin sauce and/or soy sauce on the side.

Tip: its best to layer your phó bowls with noodles, then the cabbage and herbs and then place the beef on top so that the hot broth hits the beef first. Once the broth has been added top with mung beans, spring onions, chillies, a squeeze of lime and a dash of sriracha, hoisin sauce or soy sauce.

Once everyone has filled their bowl with their preferred selection of ingredients, ladle the hot broth into the bowls. Keep any extra broth hot just in case you want a second helping! Any unused broth can be stored in the refrigerator or frozen.

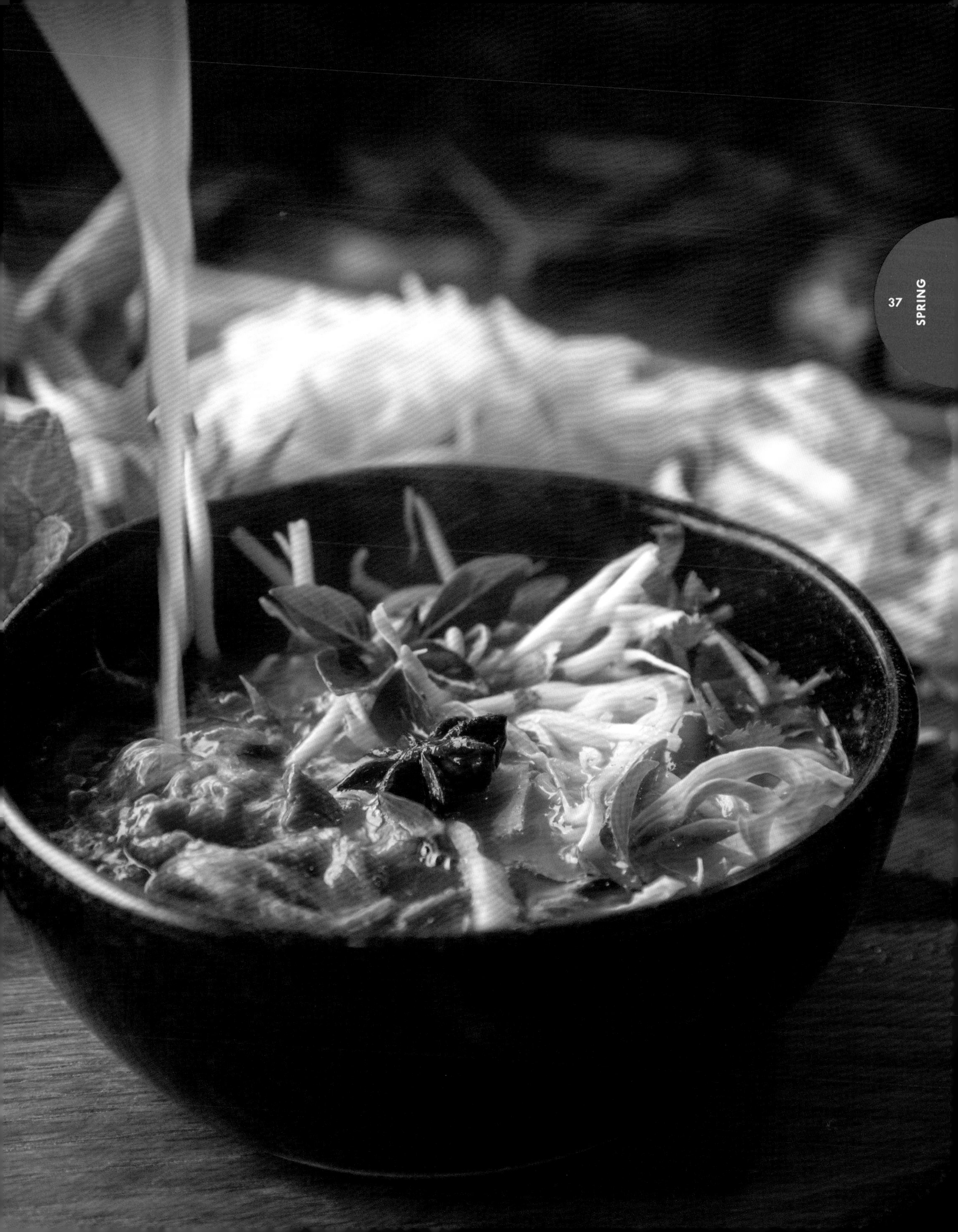

Meg's Chicken Enchiladas

Makes 10

We thought the book wouldn't be the same without another recipe from my friend Megan Dunbar, so here it is. We are lucky to have her lovely daughter, Maya Paddy now baking at the deli, which is a bonus for us as she is doing a fabulous job.

ENCHILADAS

1 lt good quality **CHICKEN STOCK**

800g **CHICKEN BREASTS**, *skin removed, sliced lengthways through the middle*

1 **ONION**, *peeled, roughly chopped*

1 **BAY LEAF**

1 tbsp **FRESH OREGANO**, *or 1½ tsp of* **DRIED OREGANO**

1 tsp **CUMIN POWDER**

3 cups (300g) **CHEESE**, *grated + some for the topping*

1 small **ONION**, *peeled, finely diced*

10 **FLOUR TORTILLAS**

¼ cup (10g) **FRESH CORIANDER**, *roughly chopped for garnish*

MEG'S RED SAUCE

3 tbsp **VEGETABLE OIL**

1½ tbsp **PLAIN FLOUR**

2 – 3 tsp **MEXICAN SEASONING POWDER** (or 1 – 2 tsp **CHILLI POWDER** or **FLAKES**)

1½ cups (275ml) **TOMATO PUREE** or **TOMATO PASSATA SAUCE**

1 tbsp **FRESH OREGANO**, *or 1½ tsp of* **DRIED OREGANO**

1 tsp **GROUND CUMIN**

SALT and freshly **GROUND BLACK PEPPER**

Note: Mexican seasoning can be quite salty so taste the sauce before adding any extra salt. If using chilli powder add a little bit at a time until you get the desired heat.

To poach the chicken: in a medium size saucepan, add the stock, chicken breasts, onion, bay leaf and oregano. Place over a medium heat and bring to the boil, cover with a lid and reduce the heat to a gentle simmer. Cook for approximately 15 minutes or until the chicken is cooked through.

Remove from the heat. Strain and reserve the broth for **MEG'S RED SAUCE**. Discard the onion and bay leaf. Set the chicken breasts aside to cool a little. When the chicken is cool enough to handle, shred the chicken into a mixing bowl.

To prepare Meg's Red Sauce: place a saucepan over medium heat and add the oil. When hot add the flour and cook for a minute, stirring constantly. Add Mexican seasoning (or chilli) and cook for 30 seconds, then stir through the reserved chicken broth, tomato puree (or passata), oregano and cumin.

Reduce the heat to very low and simmer for at least 15 – 20 minutes; the longer the sauce cooks the better it gets! Adjust seasoning to taste.

To prepare the chicken filling: add 1 cup of MEG'S RED SAUCE to the shredded chicken, along with the cumin, grated cheese and diced onion. Mix until well combined and set aside.

To prepare the enchiladas: preheat oven to 170°C.

Pour some of the remaining sauce (save a little for the top) into a large ovenproof baking dish. Place a small handful of the chicken filling onto each tortilla and roll it up. Place the tortillas into the baking dish. Spoon the remaining sauce around the sides of the tortillas and top with some grated cheese.

Bake for 20 – 30 minutes or until heated through and the cheese is melted. Remove from the oven and sprinkle over the fresh coriander. Serve with small bowls of sour cream, guacamole, and wedges of fresh lime.

Optional additions: try adding chopped jalapeños, black beans, cooked fresh corn, diced capsicum and fresh herbs to your shredded chicken mix to spice it up a bit.

Paper Baked Fish

w/

Preserved Lemon Yoghurt + Crispy Capers

Serves 4 to 6

GF

Moreish is the best way to describe these little parcels of goodness. Preserved lemons give a lovely distinct Moroccan flavour, but if you can't find them lemon zest is a good substitute.

PRESERVED LEMON YOGHURT

2 tbsp **FRESH CURLY PARSLEY**, *very finely chopped*
1 tbsp **FRESH CHIVES** or **RED ONION**, *very finely chopped*
1 **PRESERVED LEMON**, *skin only, very finely diced*
1 tbsp **FRESH LEMON JUICE**
1 clove **GARLIC**, *peeled, crushed and very finely chopped*
1 tbsp **EXTRA VIRGIN OLIVE OIL**
1 tbsp **TAHINI**
2 tsp **CUMIN SEEDS**, *toasted*
¾ cup (180ml) **NATURAL YOGHURT**
A pinch of **SALT** and freshly **GROUND BLACK PEPPER**

FISH PARCELS

BAKING PAPER, *for making the paper parcels*
600g – 800g fresh firm **WHITE FISH FILLETS**
½ cup (65g) **CAPERS**, *drained*
2 tbsp **OLIVE OIL** *(for frying the capers)*

Preheat oven to 180°C.

To prepare the preserved lemon yoghurt: in a small bowl whisk together all the ingredients until well combined.

To prepare the fish parcels: cut the baking paper into 4 – 6 pieces, approximately A4 sized. Place the individual fish fillets onto the pieces of baking paper. Spoon some of the yoghurt mixture onto each fillet. Gather up the edges of the baking paper and twist them together to form little paper parcels.

Place all the parcels on a baking tray. Bake for 6 – 10 minutes or until just cooked through.

Note: smaller fillets will take less time to cook and the fish will continue to cook once it is out of the oven, so it is a good idea to keep an eye on them and remove them just before you think they are ready.

To prepare the crispy capers: using paper towels or a clean tea towel, squeeze the capers until they are very dry. Place a wok or frying pan over a high heat and add the oil.

When the oil is really hot add the capers and cook for a few minutes until they are nice and crispy, stirring often. Remove the crispy capers and place on a paper towel to drain.

To serve: when the fish is cooked, remove the parcels from the oven and place on a serving platter. Open the parcels and sprinkle the capers over the top of the fish. Serve the remaining yoghurt sauce on the side with a leafy green salad or the *MOROCCAN CARROT SALAD (see pg 136)* and toasted pitas.

Hurry Hurry Chicken Curry

—

Kerala Chicken Curry

Serves 4 to 6

DF, GF OPTION

Amy Melchior sure knows her curries, this divine slow cooked chicken curry proves it. Indian curry leaves give this dish its distinct flavour. You can find them in big bunches in the fresh vegetable section of Asian supermarkets or health food shops – store a bunch in your freezer for future use.

Chicken Maryland is a cut of chicken that contains the thigh and drumstick. Chicken pieces or a whole chicken cut into 6 portions works well too. To make this curry gluten free substitute the malt vinegar with cider vinegar or red wine vinegar.

KERALA CURRY PASTE

3 **SHALLOTS** or 1 **RED ONION**, peeled, diced

3cm piece **FRESH GINGER**, chopped

4 **FRESH** or **DRIED RED CHILLIES**, roughly chopped

2 tbsp **CORIANDER SEEDS**, toasted

1 tbsp **CUMIN SEEDS**, toasted

1 tsp **TURMERIC POWDER**

2 tsp **GROUND CINNAMON**

2 tsp **GARAM MASALA POWDER**

6 **CARDAMOM PODS**, seeds only or 1 tsp **GROUND CARDAMOM**

½ tsp whole **BLACK PEPPERCORNS**

2 tsp **SALT**

1 tbsp **COCONUT SUGAR** or soft **BROWN SUGAR**

2 tbsp **MALT VINEGAR**

2 tbsp **VEGETABLE OIL**

¼ cup (60ml) **WATER**

KERALA CHICKEN CURRY

4 **CHICKEN MARYLANDS** cut through the joint

2 tbsp **GHEE** or **COCONUT OIL**

3 **SHALLOTS** or 1 **RED ONION**, thinly sliced

¼ tsp **BLACK MUSTARD SEEDS**

12 **CURRY LEAVES**

4 long **ASIAN EGGPLANTS**, roughly chopped into large chunks

2 cups (500ml) **CHICKEN STOCK/BROTH**

1 cup (250ml) **WATER**

To prepare the curry paste: using a food processor, blend the shallots (or onion), ginger, chillies, spices, pepper, salt, sugar and malt vinegar until well combined. Add the oil and water and blend for a few minutes until a thick paste is formed.

To marinate the chicken: place the chicken pieces into a bowl and rub ½ of the curry paste mixture over them. Set aside to marinate for at least 20 minutes or place in the refrigerator to marinate overnight.

To cook the curry: place a large flameproof casserole dish over a medium to high heat and add the ghee or oil. When hot, add the shallots or onion and cook until golden and crispy. Add the mustard seeds, curry leaves and chicken pieces. Cook for a few minutes or until the chicken is nicely browned on both sides.

Add the rest of the curry paste and stir through the eggplant. Cook for a few minutes, stirring often until the curry paste is fragrant. Add the chicken stock and the water and bring to the boil.

When boiling reduce the heat to low, cover with a tight fitting lid and cook for 40 – 50 minutes or until the chicken is cooked through. Remove from the heat and adjust seasoning to taste.

Serve with basmati rice or try it with *TURMERIC, LIME + COCONUT CAULIFLOWER RICE (see pg 226)* and the *INDIAN GREEN COCONUT CHUTNEY (see pg 247)*.

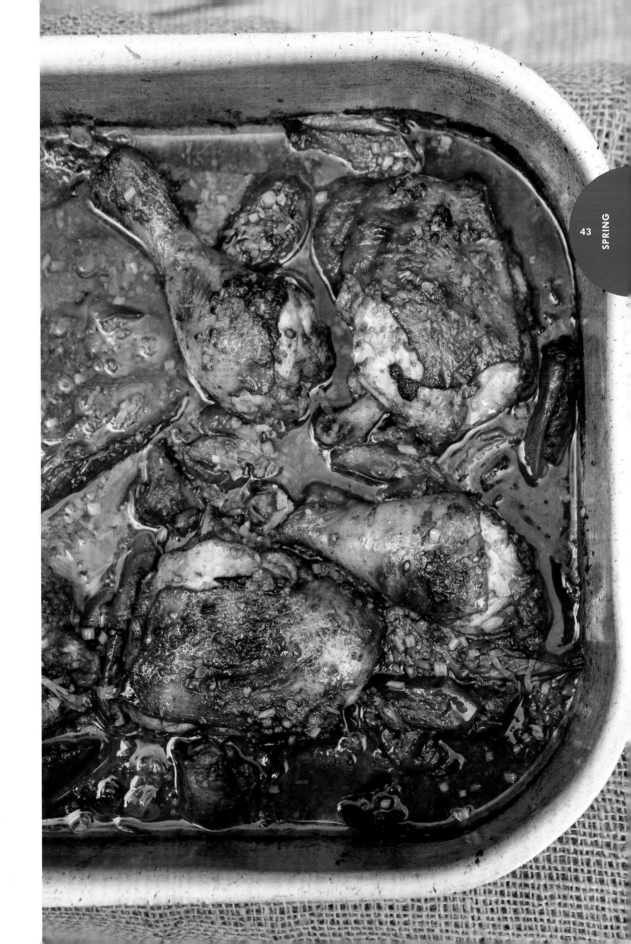

Emma's Chilli Con Carne

Serves 4 to 6

DF, GF

This lovely recipe was given to me by my good friend Emma Rasile.

The secret to a great chilli is the long and slow cooking time. Emma finds cooking chilli therapeutic – "the method and the result are good for the soul". Try to use fresh herbs if you have them, as the flavour is more aromatic.

CHILLI

4 tbsp **OLIVE OIL**
1 **ONION**, peeled, finely diced
4 cloves **GARLIC**, peeled, crushed and finely chopped
2 tsp **FRESH THYME** (or 1 tsp **DRIED THYME**)
2 tsp **FRESH OREGANO** (or 1 tsp **DRIED OREGANO**)
1 tsp each of **GROUND CUMIN**, **GROUND CORIANDER**, **GROUND GINGER**
2 tsp **PAPRIKA**
1kg **PRIME BEEF MINCE**
3 tbsp **TOMATO PASTE**
1 tbsp **GLUTEN FREE WORCESTERSHIRE SAUCE**
2 x 400g cans **DICED TOMATOES**
1½ tsp **SALT** and freshly **GROUND BLACK PEPPER**
1 x 400g can **BLACK BEANS** or **KIDNEY BEANS**, drained
1 tsp **CHILLI FLAKES** and/or **CAYENNE PEPPER**, optional, see note below

Place a large flameproof casserole dish over a medium heat. Add 2 tablespoons of the olive oil, along with the onion, garlic, herbs and spices. Cook for 5 minutes, stirring often until the onion is translucent.

Transfer the onion into a small bowl. Add the remaining oil to the casserole dish and when hot add the mince. Cook for 5 minutes breaking up the mince while it is cooking, to ensure it is evenly browned.

Add the onion mixture back into the pan, and then stir through the tomato paste, Worcestershire sauce, diced tomatoes, salt and pepper.

Cover with a tight fitting lid and reduce the heat to as low as possible. Simmer for 40 minutes, stirring every now and then. If the sauce starts to catch at all add a dash of hot water.

Add the beans and simmer for 10 minutes longer or until the beans are heated through and the sauce has reduced.

To make it hot: once you've fed the little kids or those who don't like chilli, it's time to make it hot! Stir through some Cayenne Pepper and/ or Chilli flakes; 1 teaspoon of each gives it a good kick!

To serve: Emma's Chilli Con Carne is delicious served with rice or tacos. Little side dishes of guacamole, salsa, fresh chopped coriander and yoghurt or sour cream make it the perfect meal.

For little kids Emma serves the chilli with grated carrot, cheese, iceberg lettuce, avocado and tacos.

Nutty Cacao Crunch Bar

Makes 20 small squares

DF, GF, VEGAN

This is a lovely recipe full to the brim with nutty goodness. Great as an afternoon pick me up or pop a piece into the kids' lunch box instead of a muesli bar.

Feel free to play around with the ingredients; you can easily swap out some of the nuts or seeds for dried fruit to satisfy those with more of a sweet tooth.

CRUNCH BAR

⅓ cup (50g) **COCONUT OIL**
¾ cup (225g) good quality **NATURAL PEANUT BUTTER**, we use Pic's
½ cup (140g) **GLUTEN FREE BROWN RICE SYRUP** or **MAPLE SYRUP**
1 tsp **VANILLA EXTRACT**
¼ tsp **SALT**
1 cup (140g) **NATURAL WHOLE ROASTED CASHEW NUTS**
½ cup (80g) **NATURAL WHOLE ROASTED PEANUTS**
½ cup (80g) **PUMPKIN SEEDS**, toasted
½ cup (70g) **SUNFLOWER SEEDS**, toasted
1 cup (70g) **LONG THREAD COCONUT**, toasted
½ cup (70g) **BUCKWHEAT GROATS**, raw – untoasted
½ cup (60g) **CACAO NIBS**
¼ cup (25g) **CACAO POWDER**
½ cup (80g) **CHIA SEEDS**
80g **DARK CHOCOLATE** 70% cocoa, we use Whittaker's,
1½ tbsp **VEGETABLE OIL**

Grease and line a 20 x 30cm slice tin with baking paper.

In a small saucepan over a low heat, melt together the coconut oil, peanut butter and brown rice syrup, stirring until well combined. Remove from the heat and stir through the vanilla and salt.

In a mixing bowl combine all the nuts, toasted seeds and toasted coconut, buckwheat groats, cacao nibs, cacao powder and chia seeds.

Pour the warm peanut butter mixture into the dry mixture and stir until well combined.

Press the mixture into the prepared tin and place in the refrigerator for 30 minutes to set.

Once the slice is firm to the touch, melt the chocolate and oil together by either placing the chocolate and oil into a heat proof bowl over a saucepan of simmering water, or by placing in a microwavable bowl and using a microwave set on high — melt the chocolate in short 20 – 30 second bursts until just melted. Remove from the heat and stir well until smooth.

Pour the melted chocolate over the top and spread it out so it covers the top of the slice. Place in the refrigerator for 2 hours to fully set. Cut into small pieces using a serrated knife. Store in an airtight container in the refrigerator.

The Richie Brownie

Serves 12 to 16

A legendary slice we created and named after a very special All Black.
This brownie has been a long-standing favourite at Ripe, we have been serving it up for nearly 15 years!

BROWNIE

300g UNSALTED BUTTER, diced
300g DARK CHOCOLATE BUTTONS
6 EGGS
2 cups (440g) CASTER SUGAR
1 tsp VANILLA EXTRACT
1¼ cups (190g) PLAIN FLOUR
1 cup (100g) COCOA POWDER

FILLING

1½ cups (300g) CREAM CHEESE
1¼ cups (200g) WHITE CHOCOLATE BUTTONS
1 tbsp VEGETABLE OIL

Preheat oven to 180°C.

Grease and line a 20 x 30cm high-sided slice tin with baking paper.

To prepare the brownie: melt the butter and chocolate together, by either placing the butter and chocolate into a heatproof bowl over a saucepan of simmering water, or alternatively use your microwave — melt the chocolate and butter together on a high heat, in short bursts of 20 – 30 seconds for a minute or so until just melted. Stir until well combined and set aside to cool a little.

In a large mixing bowl, using a whisk or a handheld electric beater, whisk the eggs, sugar and vanilla together for a few minutes until thick and creamy.

Sift the flour and cocoa powder over the egg mixture. Using a large metal spoon stir until smooth and glossy. Stir through the melted chocolate mixture until it is just combined.

Note: don't over mix it — that is the downfall of many a brownie!

To prepare the filling: melt the cream cheese, white chocolate and oil together using one of the methods mentioned previously. Using a whisk or handheld electric beater, mix until well combined and smooth.

Pour half of the chocolate brownie mixture into the slice tin. Using a large spoon, dollop the cream cheese mix onto the brownie. Carefully spread the cream cheese out until it covers the brownie.

Pour the remaining brownie mixture over the top. Carefully spread the brownie mixture over the top so it covers the cream cheese layer. If this is too fiddly you can just marble brownie mixture through the cream cheese.

Place in the oven to bake for 35 – 45 minutes, or until just starting to set in the middle and a glossy crust has formed. Remove from the oven and allow to cool in the tin for at least an hour before cutting.

Middle Eastern Tahini + Almond Biscuits

Makes 20 to 25 small biscuits

DF, GF, VEGAN

Delightful little biscuits full of exotic flavours, which are vegan and gluten free!

You can find brown rice flour at health stores and some supermarkets; if you are not gluten sensitive you can use plain flour instead.

BISCUITS

⅓ cup (45g) **PISTACHIOS**, *lightly toasted*
1¾ cups (175g) **GROUND ALMONDS**
3 tbsp **BROWN RICE FLOUR**
½ cup (80g) soft **BROWN SUGAR**
1 tsp **BAKING POWDER**
½ tsp **FENNEL SEEDS**
ZEST of 1 **LEMON** or **LIME** + 3 tbsp of **FRESH LEMON** or **LIME JUICE**
½ cup (125ml) **OLIVE OIL**
2 tbsp **TAHINI**
SEEDS of ½ a **VANILLA POD** or 1 tsp **VANILLA EXTRACT**

LEMON + FENNEL ICING

1 cup (150g) **ICING SUGAR**
2 tbsp **FRESH LEMON** or **LIME JUICE**
¼ tsp **FENNEL SEEDS**

Preheat oven to 180°C.

Grease and line a baking tray with baking paper.

Lightly grind or finely chop ¼ cup (35g) of the pistachios. Save the remaining pistachios for decorating the tops of the biscuits.

In a mixing bowl combine the ground almonds, pistachios, rice flour, brown sugar, baking powder and fennel seeds. Add the rest of the ingredients and mix for a few minutes until very well combined.

Roll the mixture into small walnut sized balls and place on the prepared baking tray. Press a pistachio onto the top of each ball.

Place in the oven to bake for 10 – 12 minutes or until the cookies are firm to the touch but still soft in the middle. Remove from the oven and set aside to cool.

To prepare the lemon and fennel icing: mix all the ingredients together in a small bowl. When the biscuits have cooled, dip one side of the biscuits into the icing or drizzle some over the top of each biscuit.

Go To Banana Birthday Cake

Serves 12 to 16

This banana cake is one of Amy Melchior's go to recipes when a quick and easy cake is needed. It's the perfect cake for a birthday or school fair. Amy has given this recipe to kids as young as 5 years old to make and it's turned out moist and delicious every time – it's basically fool proof.

This cake is big enough and sturdy enough to cut into two layers and fill with cream and fresh bananas. You can give this cake a decadent chocolate makeover by substituting ¼ of a cup of the flour for cocoa powder, and smothering the cake in chocolate ganache instead of the buttercream icing.

CAKE

3 large **EGGS**
1 cup (250ml) **VEGETABLE OIL**
¾ cup (120g) soft **BROWN SUGAR**
¾ cup (170g) **CASTER SUGAR**
2 tsp **VANILLA EXTRACT**
3 large ripe **BANANAS**, mashed
2 tbsp **LEMON JUICE**
2 cups (300g) **PLAIN FLOUR**
1 tsp **CINNAMON**
1 tsp **GROUND GINGER**
1 tsp **BAKING SODA**
2 tsp **BAKING POWDER**
A pinch of **SALT**

Preheat the oven to 170°C.

Grease and lightly flour a 26cm Bundt cake tin or grease and line a 26cm cake tin with baking paper.

In a small mixing bowl, using a whisk or a handheld electric beater, beat the eggs, oil, sugars and vanilla until light and creamy. Stir through the bananas and lemon juice.

In a large mixing bowl sift together all the dry ingredients. Make a well in the middle of the dry mix. Pour in the wet mixture and mix until well combined.

Pour the batter into the tin and bake for 50 – 60 minutes or until a skewer inserted into the middle comes out clean. Remove the cake from the oven and leave to cool in the tin for 10 minutes before turning out onto a wire rack.

MAPLE BUTTERCREAM ICING

80g **BUTTER**, softened
2 tbsp **MAPLE SYRUP**
1½ cups (230g) **ICING SUGAR**
1 tsp **VANILLA EXTRACT** or **CARAMEL ESSENCE**

DECORATIONS

A small handful of **HUNDREDS AND THOUSANDS** or your favourite cake decorations

To prepare the icing: using a cake mixer fitted with a balloon whisk, or using a handheld electric beater, beat the butter and maple syrup until very soft and creamy. Add the icing sugar and vanilla, or caramel essence and beat for a few minutes until light and fluffy.

To decorate the cake: place the cake onto a serving platter and spread the caramel icing over the top. Sprinkle with hundreds and thousands or decorate with your favourite cake decorations, lollies or flowers.

Coconut Frangipane

w/

Rhubarb + Star Anise

Serves 6 to 8

GF

At Ripe this beautiful fragrant frangipane tart is made with gluten free pastry, which gives it a lovely, delicate, light crust. You can use classic sweet shortcrust pastry if you are not gluten sensitive.

This gluten free pastry makes enough for one large tart or two small tarts. This wonderful recipe is from our fabulous baker Jo Singer.

If you would like to make a large 30cm round frangipane tart, just double the recipe for the rhubarb compote and frangipane mixture.

JO'S GLUTEN FREE SWEET SHORTCRUST PASTRY

1½ cups (250g) **BROWN RICE FLOUR** + extra for dusting the bench etc
¾ cup (100g) **CORNFLOUR**
⅓ cup (40g) **TAPIOCA FLOUR**
1 tsp **XANTHAN GUM**
1 tsp **BAKING POWDER**
½ tsp **SALT**
200g **CASTER SUGAR**
260g cold **UNSALTED BUTTER**, diced
2 tsp **CHIA SEEDS**
2 **EGG YOLKS** mixed with 1½ tbsp **COLD WATER**

Note: the quantity of this dough is enough to make one large 30cm round tart tin or two 13 x 30cm rectangular tarts. We recommend freezing half the dough so you have some on hand for future use.

To prepare the pastry: using a food processor, blend all the dry ingredients together until well combined. Add the diced butter and chia seeds, blend until the mixture resembles fine breadcrumbs. Add the egg yolks and water mixture, blend well for a few minutes until the mixture forms a soft dough.

Lightly flour the bench using some of the brown rice flour. Transfer the dough onto the bench and lightly knead it for a few minutes, then shape into a ball, cover and place in the refrigerator for a few hours to firm up.

You can store any unused pastry in a zip lock bag in the freezer for up to 6 months, just defrost as needed.

FRANGIPANE TART

½ x quantity of *JO'S GLUTEN FREE SWEET SHORTCRUST PASTRY*

Tip: you will need to make the pastry in advance as it needs to chill for a couple of hours in the refrigerator before you can roll it.

Or for those who are not gluten sensitive —
2 sheets of **SWEET SHORTCRUST PASTRY**, defrosted

RHUBARB COMPOTE

500g **FRESH RHUBARB**, cut into 3cm pieces
2 tbsp **WATER**
½ cup (110g) **CASTER SUGAR**
2 x **WHOLE STAR ANISE**
2 tsp **FRESH GINGER**, grated

FRANGIPANE FILLING

¾ cup (75g) **GROUND ALMONDS**
1 cup (100g) **DESICCATED COCONUT**
⅓ cup (40g) **CORNFLOUR**
A pinch of **SALT**
120g **UNSALTED BUTTER**, softened well
⅔ cup (150g) **CASTER SUGAR**
1 tsp **VANILLA EXTRACT**
1 tsp **LEMON ZEST**
2 **EGGS**

Preheat oven to 160°C.

Grease a 13 x 36cm fluted tart tin or a 20 x 30cm slice tin with melted butter.

To prepare the compote: place all ingredients in a saucepan, place over a low heat and simmer for 5 minutes or until the rhubarb is nice and soft. Remove from the heat and transfer into a small bowl. Discard the star anise, set aside to cool a little and then place in the refrigerator to cool completely.

To prepare the frangipane: in a mixing bowl, combine the ground almonds, coconut, cornflour and salt together.

Using a cake mixer or handheld electric beater, beat the butter, sugar, vanilla and lemon zest together until very creamy. Add the eggs one at a time, scraping down the sides of the bowl after each addition. Beat until light and fluffy. Add the dry mixture and beat until well combined.

Transfer the chilled ½ quantity of gluten free pastry dough on to a clean bench lightly dusted with brown rice flour. Knead for about 30 seconds to warm the dough and make it easier to roll. Dust a rolling pin with the brown rice flour and gently roll the pastry out into a rectangle that is approximately 5 mm thick. Line the greased tart tin with the pastry.

Spread ¾ of the cooled rhubarb compote over the base, reserving some for decorating the top. Using a large spoon, dollop the coconut frangipane on top. Gently spread the frangipane mixture out so it covers the rhubarb and scatter the remaining rhubarb over the top.

Place in the oven to bake for 30 – 40 minutes or until the crust is golden and the frangipane is just set. Leave in the tin to cool for at least 15 minutes before removing and serving. Serve with whipped cream or natural yoghurt.

Angie's Peanut Butter Cheesecake Slice

Serves 10 to 15

A good friend of mine, Kitch Davies, gave this recipe to me years ago. Kitch and I had great fun working together at Designers Guild in London when I first started my career.

It is extremely rich so you only need a small serving, although you will find yourself coming back for more again and again!

BASE
250g **GINGERNUT BISCUITS**
120g **BUTTER**, melted

CHEESECAKE
400g **CREAM CHEESE**, softened
100g **ICING SUGAR**, sifted
30g **BUTTER**, melted
½ tsp **VANILLA EXTRACT**
¾ cup (200g) good quality **CRUNCHY PEANUT BUTTER**, we use Fix & Fogg
1 tbsp **LEMON JUICE**
1 cup (250ml) **CREAM**

TOPPING
100g good quality **DARK CHOCOLATE**, min 60% cocoa
⅓ cup (85ml) **CREAM**
½ cup (75g) **SALTED ROASTED PEANUTS**, roughly chopped, for garnish

Grease and line a 20 x 30 cm slice tin with baking paper.

To prepare the base: using a food processor, blend the biscuits into fine crumbs. Add the melted butter and blend until well combined. Press the biscuit mixture into the prepared tin using the back of a metal spoon to flatten. Cover and place in the refrigerator for 15 minutes to firm up.

To prepare the cheesecake mixture: blend the cream cheese, icing sugar, melted butter, vanilla, peanut butter and lemon juice in the food processor until smooth and creamy. Transfer the mixture into a large mixing bowl.

In a metal bowl whip the cream until soft peaks are formed. Fold a couple of large spoons of the whipped cream into the cream cheese mix to lighten the mixture, then gently fold through the rest of the cream until it is well combined.

Spread the cheesecake mixture into the chilled base ensuring the top is nice and smooth. Place it into the refrigerator to chill while you prepare the topping.

To prepare the topping: melt the chocolate and cream together, either by placing into a heatproof bowl over a pot of simmering water, or in the microwave on high, in short 20 – 30 second bursts, until the chocolate is just starting to melt. Remove from the heat and stir together until smooth and glossy.

Spread the chocolate over the top of the slice and sprinkle with the chopped peanuts. Place in the refrigerator to set for at least 3 hours or overnight. Cut into small squares to serve.

Salted Caramel Hummingbird Layer Cake

Serves 12 to 16

*This is a true 'wow factor' 4-layer cake.
Amy Melchior created this recipe for our 'Ripe Recipe Box', but it has been so popular we felt we should include it in the book as well.*

LAYER CAKE

2½ cups (380g) **PLAIN FLOUR**
2 tsp **GROUND CINNAMON**
2 tsp **BAKING POWDER**
1 tsp **BAKING SODA**
Pinch of **FLAKY SEA SALT**
4 **EGGS**
1 cup (250ml) **VEGETABLE OIL**
1 cup (160g) soft **BROWN SUGAR**
1 cup (220g) **CASTER SUGAR**
2 tsp **VANILLA EXTRACT**
4 big **BANANAS**, mashed
1 x 420g can **CRUSHED PINEAPPLE**, well drained
1 cup (120g) **WALNUTS**, roughly chopped

SALTED CARAMEL ICING

1 cup (160g) soft **BROWN SUGAR**
1 tbsp **GOLDEN SYRUP**
1 cup (250ml) **CREAM**
½ tsp **FLAKY SEA SALT**
500g **CREAM CHEESE**

Preheat oven to 180°C.

Grease and line two x 26 cm cake tins with baking paper.

In a large bowl sift together all the dry ingredients. In a second bowl, using a whisk beat the eggs, oil, sugars and vanilla until light and creamy.

Make a well in the middle of the dry mix. Pour in the egg and oil mix. Add the mashed bananas, pineapple and half the walnuts and mix until just combined.

Divide the batter evenly between the two tins. Bake for 35 – 40 minutes or until a skewer inserted into the centre comes out clean.

Remove the cakes from the oven and leave to cool in their tins for 10 minutes before turning them out onto a wire rack to cool completely.

To make the icing: in a saucepan over a medium heat, add the brown sugar, golden syrup, cream and salt. Bring to the boil and cook for 5 minutes.

Remove from the heat and set aside to cool. Using a cake mixer or hand blender, beat the cream cheese until smooth. Add half of the caramel sauce and beat until creamy and well combined.

To assemble the cake: once the cakes are completely cooled, slice both cakes in half through the middle so you have 4 even layers. Divide the icing into four even portions. Spread a portion of icing between each layer.

Drizzle a spoon of the caramel over each layer. Spread the remaining icing on top and lightly around the sides. Drizzle over the rest of the caramel and sprinkle with the reserved walnuts.

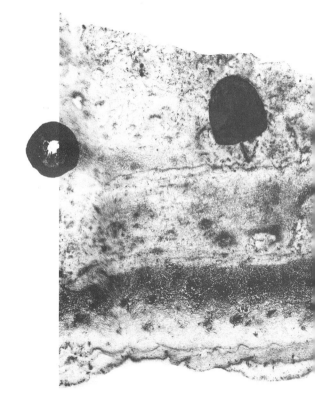

Long evenings

Ice tea

Heavenly salads

Sand and swims

Ice creams

Holidays

Cocktails on the beach

—**Summer**

Chia Summer Breakfast Puddings

Serves 4

DF, GF, VEGAN

The perfect summer breakfast, bursting with fresh fruit and healthy vibes. Another tasty creation by Jo Singer, eaten with great delight by her daughter Juna.

CHIA PUDDING

½ cup (80g) **CHIA SEEDS**
¼ cup (60ml) **MAPLE SYRUP** or **COCONUT SUGAR**
1 x 400ml can **COCONUT MILK**
1 tsp **VANILLA EXTRACT**
1 tsp **ORANGE ZEST**

OPTIONAL TOPPINGS

COCONUT YOGHURT
FRESH MINT
SEASONAL FRUIT and **BERRIES**, either fresh or poached
TOASTED COCONUT FLAKES
TOASTED NUTS
CRUNCHY GRANOLA

To prepare the chia puddings:
mix all the ingredients together, stirring well to prevent lumps. Refrigerate overnight to allow the chia seeds to swell and thicken.

To serve: give the mixture a good stir, then divide the chia pudding evenly between 4 small bowls. Top with seasonal fruit and berries, toasted coconut and toasted nuts or crunchy granola.

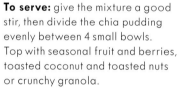

Hawaiian Poke Salad Bowls

w/

Salmon, Tuna or Tofu

Serves 4 to 6

DF, GF, VEGAN OPTION

Poke bowls are originally from Hawaii, similar to sushi but served in a bowl rather than wrapped in seaweed.

Poke is all about playing around with different vegetables and flavours. Use quinoa, or cauliflower rice instead of rice; add edamame beans or broccoli to the salad. The sky is the limit with what you can put in these delicious bowls of goodness.

PONZU SAUCE

¼ cup (60ml) **FRESH ORANGE JUICE**

¼ cup (60ml) **GLUTEN FREE TAMARI SOY SAUCE**

¼ cup (60ml) **MIRIN**

2 tbsp **COCONUT SUGAR**

3 tbsp **FRESH LIME** or **LEMON JUICE**

2 tbsp **RICE VINEGAR**

POKE SALAD

2 cups (400g) **BROWN RICE**

3 sheets **NORI SEAWEED**

400g – 600g **FRESH SALMON FILLETS** and/ or **TUNA FILLETS** (we used 300g of each), or **TOFU** diced into 2cm cubes

3 cups (300g) **RED CABBAGE** and/or **WHITE CABBAGE**, very finely sliced

1 **CARROT** and/or **BEETROOT**, peeled and grated

½ **TELEGRAPH CUCUMBER**, diced into small cubes

2 **RIPE AVOCADOS**, peeled, de-stoned and diced

1 cup (40g) **BABY SPINACH** and **KALE** or **SALAD MIX**

120g **MUNG BEAN SPROUTS** or **ALFALFA SPROUTS**

2 **SPRING ONIONS**, white and green parts, thinly sliced

ADDITIONAL TASTY TOPPINGS

PICKLED PINK GINGER, finely sliced

CRISPY FRIED SHALLOTS

JAPANESE SEAWEED SPRINKLE, store bought or make your own (see pg 240)

JAPANESE MAYO and/or **SESAME MAYO**, store bought or make your own (see pg 245)

WASABI PASTE

SRIRACHA CHILLI SAUCE

To prepare the ponzu sauce: in a clean jar whisk together all the ingredients.

Note: this recipe makes 1 cup of ponzu sauce. The ponzu will keep well in the refrigerator for at least a couple of months.

To prepare the brown rice: in a large saucepan add the brown rice and fill with water. Place over a high heat and bring to the boil.

Reduce the heat, simmering for 20 – 30 minutes or until the rice is tender. Drain through a sieve then set aside to cool a little. Transfer into a serving bowl.

To prepare the nori: lightly toast the nori sheets, either over a gas flame using metal tongs or in a frying pan over a medium heat, until crispy.

Prepare all the ingredients for the salad. Just before you are ready to serve, mix the diced salmon, tuna or tofu with ¼ cup of the ponzu dressing.

Note: if you wish to serve a combination of salmon, tuna and tofu add a couple of tablespoons of ponzu to each bowl and marinate them separately.

To serve: place the rice and marinated proteins in separate bowls. Arrange all the salad ingredients on a large platter.

Serve with a small bowl of the ponzu sauce and any or all of the tasty toppings on the side. This is a fun dish to serve as everyone gets to make their own poke bowl.

Note: many Japanese ready-made mayonnaises contain gluten so we have included recipes for a gluten free version of the Japanese and the sesame mayo (*see pg 245*).

Dan's Croquettes

Makes 12

Dan Waru has been a big part of the Ripe family for many years. These delicious croquettes are pure comfort food, perfect for a weekend brunch!

At Ripe, Dan makes his croquettes with either smoked salmon or ham and cheese. We couldn't decide on one flavour so here's both options!

CROQUETTES

1 kg **AGRIA POTATOES**, peeled, chopped in half

50g **BUTTER**

1 tsp **SALT** and freshly **GROUND BLACK PEPPER**

1 tbsp **OLIVE OIL**

1 **RED ONION**, peeled, diced

¼ cup (10g) **FRESH CURLY PARSLEY**, finely chopped

¼ cup (10g) **FRESH CHIVES**, finely chopped

1 **SPRING ONION**, white and green parts, finely chopped

¼ cup (40g) **PLAIN FLOUR**

3 **EGGS**, seasoned with salt and pepper, lightly beaten

2 cups (120g) **PANKO CRUMBS**

3 – 4 cups **VEGETABLE OIL**, for deep-frying

INGREDIENTS FOR SALMON OPTION

1 tbsp **FRESH DILL** or **FRESH CHIVES**, finely chopped

200g **FETA**, crumbled

50g **CAPERS**, finely chopped

200g **HOT SMOKED SALMON** (or any **SMOKED FISH**)

INGREDIENTS FOR HAM & CHEESE OPTION

250g **CHAMPAGNE HAM**, diced – we use the meat around the ham bone

2 cups **GRATED CHEESE**, pizza blend is best

2 tbsp **WHOLEGRAIN MUSTARD**

To prepare the potatoes: place the potatoes into a large saucepan or stockpot and fill with water. Place over a high heat and bring to the boil. Reduce the heat and cook for 20 – 30 minutes or until the potatoes are soft.

Remove from the heat and drain well. Tip the potatoes back into the saucepan. Add the butter, salt and pepper. Using a good old-fashioned potato masher, mash until smooth.

Place a small frying pan over a medium heat and add the oil and red onion. Cook for 5 minutes until translucent. Add the onion to the mashed potatoes and mix through with the herbs and spring onion.

To prepare the croquettes: add all the ingredients, for whichever option you prefer, into the mashed potato mixture. Mix until well combined. Roll the mixture into small logs or balls and place on a tray. Cover and place into the refrigerator for at least an hour (or overnight) to firm up.

To crumb the croquettes: place the flour in a flat dish, the whisked egg mix in a bowl and the breadcrumbs in another dish with high sides. Roll the croquettes in the flour, and then dip them into the egg ensuring they are completely covered in the egg.

Note: it is very important that they are well coated in the egg as this prevents them from bursting open when you deep-fry them.

Next place the croquettes into the breadcrumbs and give them a good shake to make sure they are well coated in the crumbs. Place the crumbed croquettes back into the refrigerator for 15 minutes to firm up.

To cook the croquettes: heat the oil in a wok or large saucepan. Deep-fry a few croquettes at a time, carefully turning them to ensure they brown evenly. Cook for approximately 5 minutes or until golden and crispy.

Tip: don't cook too many at once as this makes them hard to turn and it drops the temperature of the oil down, which can make the croquettes soggy! Drain well on paper towels and lightly season with salt and pepper. We serve these with *CHIPOTLE MAYO (see pg 146)*.

Summer Beets Salad

Serves 6

DF, GF, VEGAN

A sexy summer salad bursting with colour and filled with flavour. Plus its so simple and easy to make, you can whip this beauty up while you're dancing to the beets!

POMEGRANATE MOLASSES DRESSING

3 tbsp **OLIVE OIL**
2 tbsp **POMEGRANATE MOLASSES**
2 tsp **SUMAC**
2 tsp **RED WINE VINEGAR**
2 tsp **MAPLE SYRUP**
A pinch of **SALT**

SALAD

1 **CANDY BEETROOT (CHIOGGIA BEET)**, *trimmed, skin peeled, peeled into ribbons or sliced into matchsticks*
1 **PURPLE BEETROOT**, *trimmed, skin peeled, peeled into ribbons or sliced into matchsticks*
250g **CHERRY TOMATOES**, *mixed colours, cut in half*
500g **VINE TOMATOES**, *stem removed, cut into quarters*
1 **RED CAPSICUM**, *stem and seeds removed, finely sliced*
¼ cup (30g) **POMEGRANATE SEEDS** or **CRANBERRIES**

To prepare the dressing: in a small bowl, whisk together all the ingredients for the dressing.

To prepare the salad: in a large serving bowl, combine all the ingredients. Pour the dressing over the salad and gently toss to combine.

Artichoke, Tomato + Pinenut Salad

w/
Roast Olive Dressing

Serves 4 to 6

DF, GF, VEGAN

A lovely Mediterranean inspired summer salad with a delicious roast olive dressing.

ROAST OLIVE DRESSING

6 **KALAMATA OLIVES**, *pitted*
4 *tbsp* **RED WINE VINEGAR**
1 *tbsp* soft **BROWN SUGAR**
1 *tbsp* **FRESH LEMON JUICE**
½ *tsp* **DIJON MUSTARD**
3 *tbsp* **OLIVE OIL**
A pinch of **SALT** and freshly **GROUND BLACK PEPPER**

SALAD

600g small **VINE RIPENED TOMATOES**, *stem removed, cut into quarters*
½ cup (100g) **ARTICHOKES**, *roughly chopped*
3 cups (120g) **ROCKET**
½ cup (20g) **FRESH ITALIAN PARSLEY**, *roughly chopped*
½ **TELEGRAPH CUCUMBER**, *diced*
3 *tbsp* **PINENUTS**, *toasted*
½ **RED ONION**, *peeled, finely diced*

To prepare the dressing: place a small frying pan over a high heat. Add a splash of olive oil. When hot add the olives and cook for a few minutes.

Remove from the heat, and set aside to cool a little. Finely chop the olives and place them in a small bowl. Add the rest of the ingredients for the dressing and whisk until well combined.

To serve: place all the ingredients for the salad in a large serving bowl, pour the dressing over and toss to combine.

Sticky Mango + Avocado Slaw

w/

Green Lime Dressing

Serves 6 to 8

DF, GF, VEGAN

Summer is here! This slaw is the essence of summer, bursting with flavour and colour. A great slaw for a backyard barbeque or a festive feast, it's sure to be a crowd pleaser.

GREEN LIME DRESSING

¼ cup (60ml) **OLIVE OIL**
¼ cup (60ml) **CIDER VINEGAR**
½ cup (20g) **FRESH CORIANDER**, roughly chopped
¼ cup (10g) **FRESH CURLY PARSLEY**, roughly chopped
ZEST and **JUICE** of 1 **LIME**
1 tsp **DRIED OREGANO**
2 tsp **SMOKED PAPRIKA**
2 tbsp **MAPLE SYRUP** (or **HONEY**)
1 tsp **SALT**
¼ tsp freshly **GROUND BLACK PEPPER**

SLAW

3 cups (300g) **RED CABBAGE**, finely sliced
3 cups (300g) **GREEN CABBAGE**, finely sliced
1 cup (60g) **KALE** or **SPINACH**, finely sliced
½ cup (20g) **FRESH CORIANDER**, roughly chopped
1 ripe **MANGO**, skin and stone removed, diced
1 ripe **AVOCADO**, skin and stone removed, diced
1 **CAPSICUM**, stem removed, de-seeded and diced
2 **CARROTS**, peeled and grated
¼ cup (40g) **PUMPKIN SEEDS**, toasted

To prepare the dressing: place all the ingredients into a bowl. Using a stick blender, blend well until the dressing is smooth and green.

To prepare the salad: in a large serving bowl combine all the ingredients for the slaw. Pour the dressing over the slaw and mix until well combined.

Serve with the *PERUVIAN ROAST CHICKEN (see pg 146)* or *EMMA'S CHILLI CON CARNE (see pg 44).*

Almighty Eggplant

w/

Sumac

Serves 6

DF, GF, VEGAN

A delightful Middle Eastern salad of eggplant roasted in sumac, cumin, olives, tomatoes and pistachios.

SALAD

3 tbsp **OLIVE OIL**
2 **EGGPLANTS** *cut into large 4cm chunks*
1 tbsp **SUMAC**
2 tsp **CUMIN SEEDS**
1 tsp **SALT** *and freshly* **GROUND BLACK PEPPER**
1 **PRESERVED LEMON,** *skin only (flesh removed), finely diced*
½ cup (80g) **KALAMATA OLIVES**
200g **CHERRY TOMATOES,** *quartered*
½ cup (20g) **FRESH ITALIAN PARSLEY,** *roughly chopped*
3 cups (120g) **ROCKET** or **SALAD MIX**
¼ cup (40g) **ROASTED SALTED PISTACHIOS,** *roughly chopped*

BALSAMIC DRESSING

3 tbsp **BALSAMIC VINEGAR**
1 tsp **SUMAC**
2 tbsp **OLIVE OIL**
2 tbsp **MAPLE SYRUP** or **HONEY**

Preheat oven to 200°C.

Line a large baking tray with baking paper.

To roast the eggplant and olives: pour ½ of the olive oil onto the prepared tray and add the eggplant. Sprinkle over the sumac, cumin, salt and pepper. Drizzle the remaining oil over and turn to coat the eggplant in the spices.

Place in the oven to roast for 20 minutes, then add the preserved lemon and olives to the tray and cook for a further 5 -10 minutes, or until the eggplant is well roasted. Remove from the oven and set aside to cool.

To prepare the dressing: in a small jar whisk all the ingredients together.

To serve: place the roasted eggplant, preserved lemon, olives, tomatoes, and parsley in a large serving bowl.

Add the dressing and mix until well combined. Gently mix through the rocket or salad mix and sprinkle the pistachios over the top.

Sara's Pretty in Pink Salad

Serves 6

GF, VEGETARIAN

A very pretty salad created by our lovely Sara Kennedy.

We think this salad would be a stunning addition to the Christmas table.

CIDER AND MAPLE DRESSING

2 tbsp **CIDER VINEGAR**
2 tbsp **OLIVE OIL**
1 tbsp **LEMON JUICE**
2 tbsp **MAPLE SYRUP**
1 tsp **WHOLEGRAIN MUSTARD**
1 tsp **FRESH ROSEMARY**, finely chopped
A pinch of **SALT** and freshly **GROUND BLACK PEPPER**

SALAD

1 **FENNEL BULB** finely sliced, fronds reserved for garnish
1 **CUCUMBER**, peeled into ribbons
4 **RADISHES** (**WATERMELON RADISHES** if you can find them), finely sliced
1 small **PINK GRAPEFRUIT** or 2 small **BLOOD ORANGES**, peel removed, sliced into thin wedges
100g **FETA**, crumbled
3 cups (120g) **ROCKET**

To prepare the dressing: place all the ingredients into a small bowl and whisk together.

To prepare the fennel: place the sliced fennel into a bowl and pour over the cider dressing. Set aside to marinate for 15 minutes.

To serve: on a large serving platter, layer the salad starting with some of the rocket then cucumber ribbons, marinated fennel, pink grapefruit or blood orange, radish and feta. Repeat the layering then garnish with the fennel fronds.

Grilled Corn + Pineapple Summer Fiesta Salad

Serves 6 to 8

DF, GF, VEGAN

This salad is best cooked on a barbeque to nicely caramelise the pineapple and give the corn a slight smoky flavour. You can also cook it in a frying pan, just slice the corn off the cob first and then cook all the vegetables together over a medium heat. Thanks for sharing another great recipe Sara.

SALAD

6 **CORN COBS**, *husks removed*
1 **PINEAPPLE**, *peeled, cored and cut into bite sized pieces*
1 **RED ONION**, *halved, peeled and sliced into wedges*
250g **GREEN BEANS**, *tops trimmed*
2 **CHILLIES**, *finely sliced, seeds removed if you don't like it too spicy*
1 tbsp **CUMIN SEEDS**
1 tsp **SALT** *and freshly* **GROUND BLACK PEPPER**
1 cup (40g) **FRESH CORIANDER**, *finely chopped*
1 **AVOCADO**, *peeled, de-stoned and diced*
A big squeeze of **FRESH LIME** or **LEMON JUICE**

Using a barbeque grill heated to a medium heat, place the whole corn cobs along with the chopped pineapple on the grill and cook for a few minutes, turning every now and then.

Add the onion, beans, chillies and cumin. Cook for a few more minutes or until the corn turns bright yellow, the beans are tender but still crunchy and the pineapple is nicely caramelised.

Transfer the grilled pineapple, onion, beans and chillies from the barbeque onto a serving platter.

Slice the corn kernels off the cobs and mix them through the rest of the vegetables. Add the salt and pepper along with ¾ of the coriander, mix well.

Scatter the avocado and remaining coriander on top of the salad, then squeeze over the lime or lemon juice.

Bangkok Baby

—

Thai Spicy Carrot Salad

Serves 8

GF, DF

A Thai street-style carrot salad loaded with flavour and a good punch of heat. Great served with barbequed chicken or fish. This is a big recipe to feed a crowd. You can of course easily halve the recipe to feed 4, though you will find it's rather addictive and you will find yourself coming back for more!

SUMMER
80

SALAD

8 – 10 **CARROTS**, grated (you want approximately 6 cups of grated carrot)
250g **GREEN BEANS**, topped and tailed, roughly chopped
2 **SPRING ONIONS**, white and green parts, finely sliced
1 x 250g **CHERRY TOMATOES**, halved
1 cup (40g) **FRESH CORIANDER**, roughly chopped
½ cup (75g) **SALTED ROASTED PEANUTS**, roughly chopped

NAM PLAH PRIK DRESSING

3 tbsp **FISH SAUCE** (omit if vegan)
2 tbsp **RICE VINEGAR** or **WHITE VINEGAR**
2 tbsp **COCONUT SUGAR** or soft **BROWN SUGAR**
1 clove **GARLIC**, peeled, crushed and finely chopped
2 – 3 **RED CHILLIES**, finely chopped (more if you like it hot)
½ cup (125ml) **FRESH LIME JUICE**
1 tbsp **SESAME OIL**

To prepare the salad: in a large serving bowl, mix the carrots, beans, spring onions and cherry tomatoes with ½ of the coriander and peanuts.

To prepare the dressing: in a small mixing bowl combine all the ingredients and whisk together until the sugar is dissolved.

To serve: pour the dressing over the salad and mix until well combined. Scatter over the remaining coriander and the peanuts.

Berry Merry Christmas Salad

Serves 8

DF, GF, VEGAN

This is a pretty salad, all dressed up for a party in a champagne berry vinaigrette. A lovely, quick and easy salad that is perfect for the festive season.

BERRY VINAIGRETTE

125g **FRESH STRAWBERRIES**, *roughly chopped*
3 tbsp **CHAMPAGNE VINEGAR** or **WHITE BALSAMIC VINEGAR**
1½ tbsp **CASTER SUGAR**
1 tbsp **FRESH LEMON JUICE**
3 tbsp **OLIVE OIL**
A pinch of **SALT** and freshly **GROUND BLACK PEPPER**

SALAD

3 cups (120g) **ROCKET**
1 cup (40g) **FRESH BASIL**, *leaves picked*
125g **FRESH STRAWBERRIES**, *green top removed, quartered*
½ **TELEGRAPH CUCUMBER**, *diced*
500g **RIPE HEIRLOOM TOMATOES**, *core removed, cut into bite sized wedges*
½ cup (60g) **POMEGRANATE SEEDS**
1 punnet of **MICRO HERBS** with **EDIBLE FLOWERS**

To prepare the vinaigrette: place all the ingredients into a bowl and blend well using a stick blender.

To prepare the salad: in a large serving bowl or platter, combine the rocket, basil, strawberries, cucumber and tomatoes with ½ the pomegranate seeds and micro herbs.

Drizzle over some of the dressing and top with the remaining micro herbs and pomegranate seeds. Serve with the remaining dressing on the side.

Amy's Raw Fish Salad

Serves 4 to 6

DF, GF

Everyone loves a good, raw fish salad and Amy Melchior's raw fish salad is full of the flavours of summer; imagine lying in a hammock on a tropical island eating a bowl full.

If you are at all nervous of the raw factor, the fish is actually cooked by the acids in the lemon and lime juice, so it's not really raw.

We recommend using gurnard, snapper or terakihi when making this salad.

SALAD

800g **FRESH FIRM WHITE FISH FILLETS**, *skin off*
JUICE *of 2* **LEMONS**
JUICE *of 3* **LIMES**
2 tbsp **MIRIN**
2 tbsp **RICE WINE VINEGAR**
2 tbsp **COCONUT SUGAR**
4 **KAFFIR LIME LEAVES**, *very finely chopped*
2 **CAPSICUMS**, *de-seeded, finely diced*
2 **SPRING ONIONS**, *white and green parts, finely chopped*
2 ripe **AVOCADOS**, *de-stoned, peeled and cut into bite sized pieces*
½ cup (20g) **FRESH CORIANDER** *and/or* **BASIL**, *roughly chopped + some for garnish*
1 cup (250ml) **COCONUT CREAM**, *optional*
SALT *and freshly* **GROUND BLACK PEPPER**

To prepare the fish for marinating: place the fish fillets on a wooden chopping board. Using a sharp knife, thinly slice each fillet on a 90° angle, cutting against the grain of the fish.

Tip: you want the slices to be thin but not paper thin, approximately 1.5 to 2mm thick.

In a small bowl mix the lemon and lime juice with the mirin, rice wine vinegar, coconut sugar and kaffir lime leaves. Place the sliced fish fillets in a shallow dish. Pour over the lemon juice mixture.

Cover with cling film and place a weight on top, such as a small plate that fits inside the shallow dish. This ensures that all the fish is coated in the juice while it marinates.

Leave to marinate for at 30 — 40 minutes or until the fish becomes opaque and when you bite into a piece it is tender.

To serve: transfer the marinated fish and all of the marinade into a serving bowl. Add the capsicum and spring onions and gently mix through the avocado and fresh herbs.

Now you can serve it just like this, which is the way Amy prefers her raw fish or you can add the coconut cream to make a pacific style version that's creamy. Both versions are delicious.

Season to taste with salt and freshly ground black pepper.

Vegan Baked Eggplant

w/

Cashew Ricotta

Serves 6 to 8

DF, GF, VEGAN

A twist on a classic Italian dish 'eggplant involtini' that is so delicious no one will believe that it is dairy and gluten free!

We are always trying to create amazing tasting vegan dishes for our customers and this one is a winner.

BAKED EGGPLANT

2 **EGGPLANTS**, sliced lengthways – 1 cm thick
OLIVE OIL for frying
SALT and freshly **GROUND BLACK PEPPER**
1 tbsp **PINENUTS**, toasted
¼ cup (10g) **FRESH BASIL** and **FRESH ITALIAN PARSLEY**, roughly chopped

TOMATO SAUCE

2 tbsp **OLIVE OIL**
1 **ONION**, peeled, diced
4 cloves **GARLIC**, peeled, finely chopped
2 x 400g cans **DICED TOMATOES**
½ cup (125ml) **WATER**
1 tbsp **BALSAMIC VINEGAR**
½ tbsp soft **BROWN SUGAR**
1 tsp **SALT**

CASHEW RICOTTA

1 cup (140g) **CASHEW NUTS**, toasted
2 tbsp **OLIVE OIL**
2 cloves **GARLIC**, peeled, crushed and finely chopped
1 packet **SILKEN TOFU**, well drained and dried using paper towels
1 tsp **DRIED OREGANO**
1½ tsp **SALT**
ZEST of 1 **LEMON** + 2 tbsp **FRESH LEMON JUICE**
½ cup (20g) **FRESH BASIL** and **FRESH ITALIAN PARSLEY**, finely chopped
2 tbsp **PINENUTS**, toasted

Preheat oven to 180°C.

To prepare the eggplant: place a large frying pan over a high heat and add a generous splash of olive oil. Cook a few slices of eggplant at a time, fry for a minute or so on each side until nicely browned.

Repeat the process (adding more oil as needed) until all the slices are cooked. Drain the eggplant on paper towels and lightly season with salt and pepper.

To prepare the tomato sauce: place a large saucepan over a medium heat and add the olive oil. When hot add the onion and garlic and cook for a few minutes. Add the tomato, water, balsamic, brown sugar and salt.

Cook for 10 minutes, stirring every now and then. Remove from the heat and pour into a high-sided baking dish.

To prepare the cashew ricotta: using a food processor, blend the cashew nuts into fine crumbs. Add the olive oil, garlic, tofu, oregano, salt, lemon zest and juice.

Blend for a few minutes until well combined. Transfer into a bowl and stir through the fresh herbs and pinenuts.

To prepare the eggplant involtini: place a couple of heaped tablespoons of the cashew ricotta mix onto each slice of eggplant and roll it up.

Place the eggplant rolls in the tomato sauce. Scatter over the pinenuts and place in the oven to bake for 25 minutes. Sprinkle with basil and parsley just before serving.

Smoky Mumbo Jumbo Prawns

w/

Chorizo

Serves 6

GF

This dish is deliciously creamy and finger-licking good. I recently went on a trip to L.A. and San Francisco with Amy and Gemma to check out the foodie scene. This dish was served to us in a little Caribbean tapas joint. It was so delicious we had to try and recreate it for the book and I think Amy has done a pretty damn good job of it.

SMOKY PRAWNS

2 tbsp **OLIVE OIL**

2 **RED ONIONS**, peeled, halved and sliced into thin wedges

1 spicy **CHORIZO SAUSAGE**, cut in half lengthways and sliced

4 cloves **GARLIC**, peeled, crushed

3 tbsp **CAJUN SPICE MIX**

1 tbsp **SMOKED PAPRIKA**

1 tbsp **GROUND CORIANDER**

1 tbsp **GROUND CUMIN**

2 tsp soft **BROWN SUGAR**

1 x 400g can **DICED TOMATOES**

1 x 330ml bottle of **LAGER BEER**

300ml **CREAM**

600g **FRESH PRAWNS**, peeled with tail left on

A handful of **CHERRY TOMATOES**, halved

1 tsp **SALT** and freshly **GROUND BLACK PEPPER**

Place a large frying pan over a high heat and add the olive oil. When hot, add the onions, chorizo and garlic.

Cook for 5 minutes or until the chorizo is crispy. Stir through the spices, sugar and diced tomatoes then add the beer.

Reduce the heat to medium, cook for 10 minutes or until the beer and tomatoes have reduced right down to form a thick paste.

Then slowly pour in the cream while stirring continuously. Cook for a further 10 – 15 minutes or until the sauce changes to a rich orange colour.

Add the prawns, cherry tomatoes, salt and pepper, cook for a few minutes or until the prawns are just cooked through. Adjust seasoning to taste.

This dish is perfect served with chunks of fresh baguette to mop up the sauce; rice or pasta would also be yummy.

Ziva's Spicy Sticky Short Ribs

Serves 6

DF, GF

Ziva Radlovacki, our wonderful head chef at Ripe, put these delicious succulent ribs on our dinner menu. They are a hit with the crowds and finger licking good.

STICKY RIBS

2kg **BEEF SHORT RIBS**

MARINADE

1 tbsp **CUMIN SEEDS**, *toasted*
¼ cup (60ml) **GLUTEN-FREE SOY SAUCE**
2 tbsp **SAMBAL OELEK**
2 tbsp **SESAME OIL**
2 tbsp **GINGER**, *grated*
2 tbsp **FRESH LEMON JUICE**
½ cup (125ml) **MAPLE SYRUP** or *soft* **BROWN SUGAR**
SALT and *freshly* **GROUND BLACK PEPPER**

To prepare the ribs: place the rack of ribs on a chopping board and slice into individual ribs.

In a large mixing bowl (one that is big enough to fit all the ribs), mix all the ingredients for the marinade together. Add the ribs and turn to coat in the marinade.

Cover and place in the refrigerator to marinate for at least 3 hours or overnight.

To cook the ribs: preheat oven to 170°C.

Place the ribs, meaty side down with all of the marinade in a large baking tray. Cover with a piece of baking paper and wrap tightly in foil. Place in the oven to cook for 4 hours.

After 4 hours remove the foil and paper. Using tongs, flip the ribs so they are meaty side up and baste well with the sauce.

Cook for a further 15-20 minutes or until the ribs are nicely browned. Remove from the oven and season to taste. Serve with rice or boiled potatoes and lots of freshly steamed greens.

Summer | Ripe Recipes – A Third Helping

Barbeque Eye Fillet Stuffed

w/

Olive Tapenade

+ Pancetta

Serves 10 to 12

DF, GF

This is an absolutely divine tasting eye fillet. Cook it on a wood fired barbeque if you can for that extra special wood smoked flavour.

EYE FILLET

1 x whole **BEEF EYE FILLET**
250g **PANCETTA**
A roll of **NATURAL FIBRE STRING** *for trussing the beef*
SALT *and freshly* **GROUND BLACK PEPPER**

OLIVE TAPENADE

1 cup (180g) **KALAMATA OLIVES**, *pips removed*
2 tbsp **CAPERS**
3 cloves **GARLIC**, *peeled, finely chopped*
3 **ANCHOVY FILLETS**
½ cup (20g) **FRESH BASIL**, *roughly chopped*
2 tbsp **FRESH OREGANO**, *roughly chopped*
1 tbsp **FRESH ROSEMARY**, *roughly chopped*
  + a few sprigs for the stuffing
1 tbsp **FRESH LEMON JUICE**
¼ cup (60ml) **OLIVE OIL**
A pinch of **SALT** *and freshly* **GROUND BLACK PEPPER**

To prepare the eye fillet: place the eye fillet on a large wooden chopping board and trim off any sinew and fat. Cut a deep slit along the length of the fillet, but leaving the ends uncut, to create a pocket-like opening in the beef.

To prepare the tapenade: place a frying pan over a high heat with a splash of olive oil. When hot add the olives and fry for 3 – 4 minutes.

Remove from the heat and allow to cool. Using a food processor, blend all the ingredients together until lightly combined. Transfer into a small bowl.

To stuff and truss the beef: open the pocket in the beef and evenly spread half of the tapenade inside the beef.

Lay 6 pieces of the pancetta inside the pocket so they are covering the length of the inside of the beef fillet. Close the pocket and wrap the remaining pancetta around the outside of the beef.

Cut 6 pieces of string approximately 15cm long. Wrap the string around the beef to secure the pancetta in place. Liberally drizzle olive oil all over the fillet and season really well with salt and freshly ground pepper. Wedge the sprigs of rosemary under the string.

To cook the beef: heat your barbeque to a high heat and sear the fillet for a few minutes on all sides. Now reduce the heat or move it to the coolest section of the grill.

Slow roast the fillet on the barbeque for approximately 25 – 35 minutes (depending on how rare you like your beef), turning it once during the cooking time to ensure the meat cooks evenly.

Remove from the heat and allow the beef to rest for 10 minutes before slicing. Serve with the remaining tapenade on the side.

Ripe's Manuka Hot Smoked Salmon

Serves 12 to 16

DF, GF

We serve hot smoked salmon in our Ripe Christmas Feast menu (and of course throughout the year in our cabinet) – it always gets rave reviews, so we thought we would share the love. This dish is great to serve at large parties, barbeques and family gatherings throughout the year – you don't have to wait for Christmas!

If you want to make a smaller amount just halve the recipe and reduce the size of the salmon fillet.

If you don't have a smoker at home we have listed various other options for cooking the salmon in the recipe, including simply baking it, which is also delicious.

SMOKED SALMON

1 x whole **SALMON FILLET**, *skin on, bone out*

MARINADE

½ cup (80g) soft **BROWN SUGAR**
3 tsp **HIMALAYAN PINK SALT** or **SEA SALT** (don't use iodised salt!)
2 tsp **FENNEL SEEDS**
1 tsp **CUMIN SEEDS**
2 tsp **POMEGRANATE MOLASSES**
½ cup (125ml) **FRESH ORANGE JUICE**
¼ cup (60ml) **FRESH LEMON JUICE**

GLAZE

½ tsp **SMOKED PAPRIKA**
½ tsp **CUMIN** and **FENNEL SEEDS**
3 tbsp **MAPLE SYRUP** or **HONEY**
2 tbsp **FRESH LEMON JUICE**

To prepare the salmon: place the salmon fillet onto a chopping board and run your fingers along the flesh feeling for bones; if any are found, remove them using tweezers.

To prepare the marinade: in a mixing bowl combine all the ingredients for the marinade. Mix well until all the sugar and salt has dissolved.

Using a dish that is large enough to fit the salmon fillet, pour the marinade into the dish and place the salmon fillet fleshy side down in the marinade.

Cover and place in the refrigerator for at least 4 hours or preferably overnight. Discard the marinade when you are ready to smoke the salmon.

To prepare the glaze: mix all the ingredients for the glaze together and brush a little of it over the salmon.

To smoke the salmon using a smoker: place a piece of foil in the bottom of the smoker, sprinkle a handful of Manuka wood chips on top. Place a metal wire rack on top of the wood chips.

Lay the salmon fillet skin side down on the rack – you may need to trim the salmon tail to fit it in. Place the smoker over a low heat either using the fuels or a barbeque. Cover and smoke for 15 minutes, then remove the lid and baste with the glaze every few minutes until just cooked through.

Smoking the salmon without a smoker: using an old metal roasting dish (one you don't mind tarnishing), line the bottom with foil, add a handful of Manuka wood chips and place a wire rack on top (like one you would use for cooling cakes on). Place the salmon on top of the wire rack. Cover the top of the dish with foil tightly sealing the sides.

Place the dish over a low heat on the barbeque or on the stovetop. Smoke for 15 minutes, then remove the foil and baste with the glaze every few minutes until just cooked through.

If you are doing this inside, be aware it will get quite smoky, so make sure you have all the windows and doors open, or your extractor fan on high!

Baking the salmon: preheat oven to 200°C.

Line a baking dish with foil. Place the salmon into the dish and bake for 15 minutes. After 15 minutes of cooking start basting the salmon every now and then with the glaze until the salmon is just cooked through.

To serve: place on a serving platter. For a lovely Christmas feel, sprinkle with pomegranate seeds or toasted almond flakes and fresh herbs.

This salmon is delicious served hot or cold. Any leftovers can be flaked through a salad, or try using it in Dan's Croquettes for a delicious Boxing Day brunch!

Mark's Mighty Mussels

I met Mark Lane many moons ago. At the time he was cheffing at 'Le Pont De La Tour' in London. He returned to NZ and was appointed Executive Chef at 'Hammerheads' restaurant and many others since. I am lucky that he helps us out these days at Ripe along with running his own catering company.
I love mussels and thought it would be great to have a couple of Mark's recipes for them in the book, as he is brilliant with seafood.
Thanks Mark!

Chorizo + Tomato Mussels

Serves 4

DF, GF

1kg **MUSSELS**, cleaned, de-bearded
¼ cup (60ml) **OLIVE OIL**
2 spicy **CHORIZOS**, sliced
1 **ONION**, peeled, finely diced
6 cloves **GARLIC**, peeled, finely chopped
150ml **WHITE WINE**
1 x 400g can **CHOPPED TOMATOES**,
  drained in a sieve, reserving the flesh only
5g (or a few sprigs) **FRESH THYME**, leaves
1 **RED CHILLI**, finely sliced
½ cup (20g) **FRESH ITALIAN PARSLEY**,
  chopped
A handful of **CHERRY TOMATOES**
SALT and freshly **GROUND BLACK PEPPER**

To prepare the mussels: clean and de-beard the mussels using a metal scourer or blunt knife.

To cook the mussels: using a large saucepan, or flameproof casserole dish with a lid, place over a medium heat and add the oil. When hot, add the chorizo and cook until slightly browned and crispy. Remove from the pan and set aside.

Add the onion and garlic to the pan, cooking for a few minutes and stirring often until the onion is translucent. Add the wine, bring to the boil and cook until the wine has reduced by half. Stir in the tomatoes, thyme and chilli, reduce the heat and gently simmer for 10 minutes stirring occasionally.

Add the mussels to the pan, cover with a lid and bring to the boil. Cook the mussels until the shells pop open, shaking the pot occasionally as they cook.

Remove any opened mussels from the pan (to keep them tender and juicy) and place them onto a serving dish. Continue cooking the rest of the mussels until they are all open. Transfer all the cooked mussels to the serving dish.

Add the chorizo, parsley and cherry tomatoes into the sauce and cook for a few minutes to allow the spices from the chorizo to infuse with the sauce.

Season to taste with salt and pepper. Ladle the sauce over the mussels and serve with toasted garlic bread.

South East Asian Mussels

Serves 4

DF, GF

1kg **MUSSELS**
1 tsp **SESAME OIL**
1 tbsp **COCONUT OIL**
4 **SPRING ONIONS**, finely sliced
2 cloves **GARLIC**, peeled, finely sliced
2 cm piece **FRESH GINGER**, peeled, finely
  chopped
¼ cup (10g) **FRESH CORIANDER**, stems and
  roots finely sliced, leaves picked for garnish
1 stick **LEMONGRASS**, cut into 8 pieces
2 **KAFFIR LIME LEAVES**
50g **BALINESE RUB** (see pg 235)
  or your favourite
  SOUTH EAST ASIAN CURRY PASTE
1 x 400ml can **COCONUT MILK**
40g **COCONUT SUGAR** or **PALM SUGAR**
2 tbsp **FISH SAUCE**
1 **LIME**, quartered
¼ cup (10g) **FRESH MINT LEAVES**
¼ cup (10g) **FRESH BASIL LEAVES**
50g **FRESH COCONUT**, shaved and toasted
  (optional or you could use coconut chips)

To prepare the mussels: clean and de-beard the mussels using a metal scourer or blunt knife.

To cook the mussels: using a large saucepan, or flameproof casserole dish with a lid, place over a medium heat and add the oils, spring onions, garlic, ginger, coriander stems and root, lemongrass and kaffir lime leaves.

Cook for a few minutes, stirring often until the onions are translucent. Add the curry paste and cook for a further minute. Then add the coconut milk, sugar and fish sauce and bring to the boil.

When boiling, add the mussels to the pan and cover with a lid. Cook the mussels until the shells pop open, shaking the pot occasionally as they cook.

Remove any opened mussels from the pan (to keep them tender and juicy) and place them onto a serving dish. Continue cooking the rest of the mussels until they are all open.

Transfer the mussels and the sauce onto the serving dish, squeeze over the fresh lime juice, sprinkle with the coriander leaves, mint, basil and the fresh toasted coconut.

Hazelnut Chocolate Mousse Cake

w/

Strawberries

Serves 12 to 16

DF, GF, VEGAN

This is true decadence! A sliver of this cake will satisfy all chocoholics – think hazelnut nutella dreaminess combined with dark chocolate and strawberries.

This divine mousse cake is vegan so we have used silken tofu to help bind the flavours and give it a lovely light creaminess – but don't fear the tofu, you can't taste it at all and no one will know it's in there.

BASE

100g good quality **VEGAN DARK CHOCOLATE** (at least 60% cocoa)
4 tbsp **COCONUT OIL**
50g **HAZELNUTS**
1¼ cup (125g) **GROUND ALMONDS**
100g **PRUNES**, finely chopped
2 tbsp **COCOA POWDER**
A pinch of **SALT**

CHOCOLATE MOUSSE

120g **HAZELNUTS**
2 tbsp **COCONUT OIL**
½ cup (125ml) **COCONUT CREAM**
200g good quality **VEGAN DARK CHOCOLATE** (at least 60% cocoa)
350g **SILKEN TOFU**, well drained and patted dry with paper towels
2 tbsp **COCOA POWDER**
2 tsp **VANILLA EXTRACT**
4 tbsp **MAPLE SYRUP**

TOPPING

1 tbsp **HAZELNUTS**
350g **STRAWBERRIES**, tops removed, sliced
1 – 2 tbsp **MAPLE SYRUP**

Grease a 23cm spring-form cake tin with coconut oil and line the sides with baking paper.

To toast the hazelnuts: preheat oven to 180°C.

Note: there are 3 measurements of hazelnuts in this recipe – the base, the filling and the topping.

Place all the hazelnuts used in the recipe (170g which is approximately 1¼ cups of hazelnuts) on a baking tray and roast them for about 8 – 10 minutes, or until they are lightly browned. Don't overcook them as they will continue to cook when they are out of the oven. Remove from the oven and allow to cool. Rub the skins off using a clean tea towel, don't worry if some of the skins stay on, they will still be delicious.

To prepare the base: melt the coconut oil and chocolate together, either in the microwave oven at 30 second intervals or in a heatproof bowl over a pot of simmering water. Once melted, stir until well combined.

In a blender or food processor, place the toasted hazelnuts, ground almonds, prunes, cocoa powder and salt and blend. Add the melted chocolate and blend again until well combined. Transfer the mixture into the prepared spring form tin. Press the mixture firmly and evenly into the bottom of the tin. Place in the freezer for 10 minutes to set.

To prepare the chocolate mousse: using one of the methods listed above melt the coconut oil, coconut cream and chocolate together, stirring until well combined

Place the toasted hazelnuts into a food processer and blend until fine crumbs are formed – be careful not to turn them into nut butter! Add the tofu and cocoa powder; blend for a few minutes until well combined.

Add the melted chocolate mixture, vanilla extract and maple syrup to the blender with the hazelnut mixture. Blend until well combined and smooth, scraping down the inside of the bowl with a spatula as needed. Pour the mixture onto the base. Place in the refrigerator to set for at least an hour.

To decorate and serve: remove from the tin and place on a serving platter. For a soft mousse texture let the cake come to room temperature before serving. Arrange the sliced strawberries on top, sprinkle over the hazelnuts and drizzle with maple syrup.

Lynn's Pretty Pistachio Cake

w/

Plum

Serves 10 to 12

GF

A truly delicious cake created by our lovely head baker, Lynn Colbert. It's one of those cakes that is simple to make and tastes amazing.

PISTACHIO CAKE

½ cup (70g) **PISTACHIOS**, finely chopped or ground

1¾ cups (175g) **GROUND ALMONDS**

½ cup (65g) **PLAIN GLUTEN FREE FLOUR**, we use Bakels or Edmonds

1½ tsp **BAKING POWDER**

A pinch of **SALT**

250g **UNSALTED BUTTER**, softened

1 cup (220g) **CASTER SUGAR**

1 **VANILLA POD**, seeds only (or 2 tsp **VANILLA EXTRACT**)

ZEST of 1 **LIME**

4 **EGGS**

2 **FRESH PLUMS** or canned **PLUMS**, pips removed, finely diced

½ cup (14g) **FREEZE-DRIED SLICED PLUMS**

ICING

1¾ – 2 cups (270g – 300g) **ICING SUGAR**

1 tbsp **FREEZE DRIED PLUMS**, crushed into a powder

1 – 2 **FRESH PLUMS** or canned **PLUMS**, pips removed, very finely diced

1 – 2 tbsp **LIME JUICE**

GARNISH

A small handful **PISTACHIOS**, roughly chopped

A small handful of **FREEZE-DRIED SLICED PLUMS** or a couple of **FRESH** or canned **PLUMS**, thinly sliced

Preheat oven to 180°C.

Grease and line a 23cm or 26cm spring-form cake tin with baking paper.

To prepare the cake: in a mixing bowl combine the pistachios, ground almonds, gluten free flour, baking powder and salt.

Using a cake mixer or handheld electric beater, cream the butter and sugar together until very light and fluffy. Add the vanilla seeds and lime zest and beat until well combined.

Add the eggs one at a time, beating well after each addition. Scrape down the inside of the bowl to ensure the eggs are well incorporated. Fold through the dry ingredients and then fold through the fresh or canned plums and the freeze-dried plums.

Transfer the cake batter into the prepared tin and bake for 45 – 60 minutes or until the cake is springy to the touch and a skewer inserted into the centre comes out clean. Remove from the oven and allow the cake to cool for 10 minutes before turning it out onto a wire rack.

To prepare the icing: place all the ingredients into a small bowl and mix until well combined. If the icing is a little thick add a little more lime or if too thin add a little more icing sugar.

To assemble the cake: transfer the cake onto a serving dish. Spread the icing over the top and place in the refrigerator for 5 – 10 minutes for the icing to set.

To serve: sprinkle with pistachios and pieces of freeze dried plums — crush some of the freeze-dried plums in your hand and scatter over the top, this will give the cake a lovely dark red dusting of plum and a burst of rich plum flavour. Serve with natural yoghurt or whipped cream.

Jude's Chocky Rocky Road

Makes 16 to 20 small squares

One of the best Christmas presents I have received the last couple of years is this Rocky Road from my friend Jude Mewburn. I was stoked when she was happy to share the recipe, as I think it's a wonderful easy present to make for friends and family. This slice is also a great idea for a school fair, or as a tasty after dinner treat.

For best results use a good quality chocolate; we recommend Whittaker's chocolate.

You can make this with any combination of nuts & fruits, so here is a base recipe and some ideas from Jude for combinations, but by all means use your own creative ideas; it would be hard to go wrong.

ROCKY ROAD

2 x 250g blocks of good quality **CHOCOLATE**, *white, milk or dark, roughly chopped*
1 tbsp **COCONUT OIL**
¾ cup of your favourite **NUTS**
½ cup **DRIED FRUIT** *or 1 cup* **NATURAL FRUIT JUBES** *or* **TURKISH DELIGHT**
½ cup **DRIED SHAVED COCONUT** *or* **LONG THREAD COCONUT**
150g **MARSHMALLOWS**
1 cup **SHORTBREAD** *or your favourite biscuit, broken into small pieces (optional)*

Note: these are Jude's recommended combinations.

- Dark chocolate, white marshmallows, hazelnuts (roasted and skins removed), Turkish delight and coconut.
- White chocolate, pink marshmallow, macadamia nuts roughly chopped, shortbread, dried cranberries, and coconut.
- Milk chocolate, marshmallows, whole almonds, natural berry bliss jubes, biscuits and coconut.

Line a 20 – 30cm slice tin with baking paper

Melt the chocolate in a heatproof bowl over a pan of simmering water. When melted, stir in the coconut oil. Set aside for 5 minutes to allow the chocolate to cool a little.

Add the nuts, dried fruits or jubes, coconut, marshmallows and shortbread (if using), into the melted chocolate and mix until well combined. Pour into the tin, distributing the marshmallows evenly in the tray!

Place in the refrigerator for 2 – 3 hours to set. Once set cut into small pieces or long strips. Store an airtight container in the refrigerator.

For gifts cut the rocky road slice into small blocks and place into cellophane bags. Tie the top of the bag with a pretty ribbon to seal it.

Ruby's Pear + Plum Spice Cake

Serves 10 to 12

Ruby Wheeler was a lovely addition to the Ripe team, her enthusiasm for baking was contagious. Ruby has now moved on to start her own baking adventure.

This recipe is based on a traditional Armenian nutmeg cake, with an amazing crunchy base. A lovely, lightly spiced cake with pear, topped with a tart plum glaze. The glaze could be made with tinned plums too and of course the cake without the glaze is perfectly delicious.

SPICE CAKE

2¼ cups (360g) soft **BROWN SUGAR**

2¼ cups (340g) **SELF-RAISING FLOUR**

2 tsp **GROUND GINGER**

1 tsp freshly grated **NUTMEG**

150g cold **BUTTER**, diced

1 cup (250ml) **MILK**

1 **EGG**

1 tsp **VANILLA EXTRACT**

1 tsp **BAKING SODA**

1 tbsp **WARM WATER**

1 firm **PEAR**, core removed, sliced into small wedges

PLUM GLAZE

8 **DORIS PLUMS** or **RED PLUMS**, quartered

2 tbsp **WATER**

3 – 4 tbsp soft **BROWN SUGAR**, add less sugar if your plums are sweet

GARNISH

A few **FREEZE DRIED PLUMS** or **FRESH PLUMS**

Preheat oven to 165°C.

Grease and line a 23cm spring-form cake tin with baking paper.

Using a food processor, blend the sugar, flour, ginger, nutmeg and butter until the mixture resembles fine breadcrumbs. Pour the dry mixture into a bowl.

Scoop 2 cups of the dry mixture out of the bowl and place it in the bottom of the cake tin. Lightly flatten the mixture so it's evenly spread out in the tin.

Using the food processor again, blend the milk, egg and vanilla.

Mix the baking soda with a tablespoon of warm water and add it to the blender, pulse to combine. Add the remaining dry mixture and blend until combined. Pour the wet mixture over the dry mixture in the tin.

Place the pear wedges so they are evenly spaced apart like a star, with the thin end of the pear wedges poking out of the cake batter and resting on the side of the cake tin.

Bake for 60 minutes or until a skewer inserted into the middle comes out clean. Remove from the oven and allow to cool in the tin for 10 minutes.

To prepare the plum glaze: in a small saucepan place the chopped plums, water and brown sugar. Place over a medium heat and cook for 10 minutes or until the plums are very soft and most of the liquid has evaporated.

Place a sieve over a bowl and pour the plums into the sieve. Using a spatula push the plums through the sieve, scraping the underside of the sieve as you go, until you have a fine smooth puree of plum for glazing the cake.

To serve: place the cake onto a serving platter. Spread the glaze over the top of the cake and decorate with some freeze-dried plum or fresh plum slices. Serve warm with whipped cream or natural yoghurt.

The G.M's Tiramisu Layer Cake

Serves 16

*Our wonderfully creative, vivacious, compassionate and inspiring general manager, Gemma Heffernan, created this amazingly rich and decadent layer cake for the book.
It's a bit of an extravagant number that would be perfect for a special occasion.*

Gemma's words of wisdom are "Do not be put off by the many steps or Swiss meringue icing – if I can do it so can you! Just believe in yourself and do not let the cake get the better of you. Just like a horse, a cake can smell fear!"

So go on, take the plunge – make the most incredible cake you have ever made, and hey, if you get stuck just give Gemma a call at Ripe, she is a great guidance counsellor on cakes and horses!

SPONGE CAKE

1 cup (160g) soft **BROWN SUGAR**
½ cup (110g) **CASTER SUGAR**
1½ tsp **GROUND CINNAMON**
½ tsp **COCOA POWDER**
¾ tsp **BAKING POWDER**
1½ cups (230g) **SELF-RAISING FLOUR**
225g **UNSALTED BUTTER**, well softened
4 large **EGGS**
2 – 4 tbsp **FRESH CREAM**

WHIPPED CREAM

400ml **FRESH CREAM**

SWISS MERINGUE
BUTTERCREAM ICING

200ml **EGG WHITES**, approximately 5 – 6
    egg whites, at room temperature
400g (1¾ cups + 2 tsp) **CASTER SUGAR**
675g **BUTTER**, at room temperature, diced
400g **MASCARPONE**
6 tbsp **KAHLUA**
2 tsp **VANILLA EXTRACT**

COFFEE SYRUP

3 tbsp **BOILING WATER**
4 tbsp **INSTANT COFFEE**
¾ cup (180ml) **KAHLUA**

GANACHE

100g good quality **DARK CHOCOLATE**,
    60% cocoa, finely chopped or grated
4 tbsp **FRESH CREAM**

Note: the Swiss meringue icing used in this recipe makes more than enough icing for this cake, so you will have plenty for future use. Left over icing can be stored in a zip lock bag and frozen for up to 3 months. Just defrost the icing, bring it to room temperature, then give it a light whip and it's ready to use on your next masterpiece.

Preheat oven to 180°C.

Grease and line 2 x 20cm or 2 x 23cm spring-form cake tins with baking paper.

To prepare the sponges: using a food processor, blend together the sugars, cinnamon, cocoa, baking powder and flour. Add the softened butter and eggs, blending until smooth and well combined.

With the motor running add just enough cream (a tablespoon at a time) to achieve a runny, smooth, dropping consistency. Divide the batter evenly between the two cake tins and bake for 20 – 25 minutes or until golden and springy to touch. Remove the sponge cakes from the oven and leave to cool.

To prepare the whipped cream: using an handheld electric beater, or cake mixer fitted with a balloon whisk, whip your cream until soft peaks have formed, and set aside in the refrigerator.

To prepare the Swiss meringue buttercream: place the clean metal mixing bowl from your cake mixer in the refrigerator to chill for 10 – 15 minutes.

Note: the reason for chilling the metal bowl is that once you have finished melting the sugar into the egg whites they are very hot. This process helps to drop the temperature of the hot egg whites, making them easier to whip.

Tip: egg whites will not whip if they come into contact with any fats or grease, so make sure all bowls and whisks are very clean.

Using another large, clean, metal mixing bowl, lightly whisk together the sugar and the egg whites. Place the bowl over a large saucepan that is ¼ filled with water.

Note: you don't want the water to touch the base of the bowl at any point while the water is simmering, so check that the base of the bowl is high enough to avoid the simmering water.

Place over a low heat and continue to gently whisk the mixture until all the sugar has completely dissolved and the egg whites are frothy. This should take approximately 10 – 15 minutes. When the mixture is hot to the touch and no sugar granules are visible it's ready for the next step.

Remove the chilled cake mixer bowl from the refrigerator and pour the hot sugar and egg whites into the bowl. Using your cake mixer, fitted with a balloon whisk, beat for 15 – 20 minutes or until the meringue mixture is fluffy, glossy and completely cool.

Tip: to test if the meringue is cool, remove the bowl from the machine and feel the base of the bowl — if it's cool to the touch it is ready.

Note: if the meringue is still warm just keep beating until it is cold — you don't want to add the butter to warm meringue otherwise it will melt the butter!

With the motor running on high, add approximately a tablespoon of the cubed butter at a time — dropping the individual cubes in to the meringue one at a time. Make sure you allow each addition of butter to fully emulsify into the meringue before adding the next tablespoon of butter.

Continued on next page...

Tip: keep a quarter of the total measure of butter out on the bench and the rest in the fridge, bringing more of the butter to room temperature as it is needed.

Continue this process, beating for approximately 15 – 20 minutes until all the butter is incorporated into the meringue, and then beat for a further 5 minutes or until the meringue mixture is very soft, fluffy and velvety.

Tip: if the mixture turns runny and soupy that means the butter is too warm! Stop and place the bowl in the refrigerator for 20 minutes to chill and chill your remaining butter for a few minutes too. Then carry on from where you left off and keep whipping.

Once the meringue icing is light and fluffy, using the paddle attachment on your cake mixer, gently mix the mascarpone, Kahlua and vanilla through the meringue until just combined – don't over mix it.

Note: you can store your Swiss meringue buttercream icing in the refrigerator until you are ready to assemble your cake – just let it come to room temperature and give it a gentle whip before using it.

Well done, you have mastered the hardest part! Now pour yourself a Kahlua and give yourself a pat on the back and take a well-earned little breather before embarking on the next steps.

To prepare the coffee syrup: in a small jug mix the freshly boiled water with the coffee and then stir in the Kahlua.

To prepare the ganache: melt the chocolate and cream together, either in a heatproof bowl, over a saucepan of simmering water on a medium heat, or use your microwave on a high heat, in short bursts of 30 seconds for a minute or so, until just melted.

Stir the ganache until it is smooth and glossy, then add ⅓ cup (85ml) of coffee syrup and mix until well combined. Set aside for a few minutes to allow the ganache to thicken to a spreadable consistency.

Tip: if it's hot in the kitchen you may need to pop the ganache in the refrigerator for 5 minutes to thicken it up.

To assemble the cake: using a serrated bread knife, slowly and carefully so you get them as even as possible, cut each sponge cake into two even layers. Place the layers on cardboard cake disks or flat metal trays.

Place 1½ cups of the Swiss meringue buttercream icing into a piping bag fitted with a wide nozzle. Place the bottom layer of one of the sponge cakes onto a serving plate (or a cardboard cake disk).

Pipe a thick, even wall of icing around the inside edge of the sponge cake to prevent the whipped cream and ganache from spilling out between the layers.

Inside the wall of icing, evenly drizzle 3 tablespoons of coffee syrup over the cake, and then spread over ⅓ of the ganache and top with ⅓ of the whipped cream.

Repeat this whole process of layering the sponge, making the piped wall of icing, adding the coffee syrup, ganache and whipped cream etc two more times. Then place the last layer of sponge cake on top and drizzle over the remaining coffee syrup. Place the cake in the refrigerator for 10 minutes to firm up.

To prepare the crumb coat: this is a thin smooth layer of the Swiss meringue buttercream icing used to set the layers of sponge cake in place and prevent any crumbs forming in the final layer of icing.

Place approximately 1 cup of the icing into a small bowl. Using a metal cake spatula lightly spread the icing thinly over the top of the cake and around the outside of the cake.

Use the icing to fill in any gaps between the layers, then scrape off any excess icing until the icing is uniform and even. Place the cake in the refrigerator for 20 minutes to firm up and to set the icing.

To prepare the cake for the final icing and decorating: using a metal cake spatula spread some of the remaining Swiss meringue butter cream icing around the outside of the cake and some across the top, until it is evenly covered and is nice and smooth.

Using the piping bag, pipe little pillow- like mounds of icing over the top and dust with a little cocoa powder.

You can store this cake in the refrigerator until you are ready to serve. Bring to room temperature before serving.

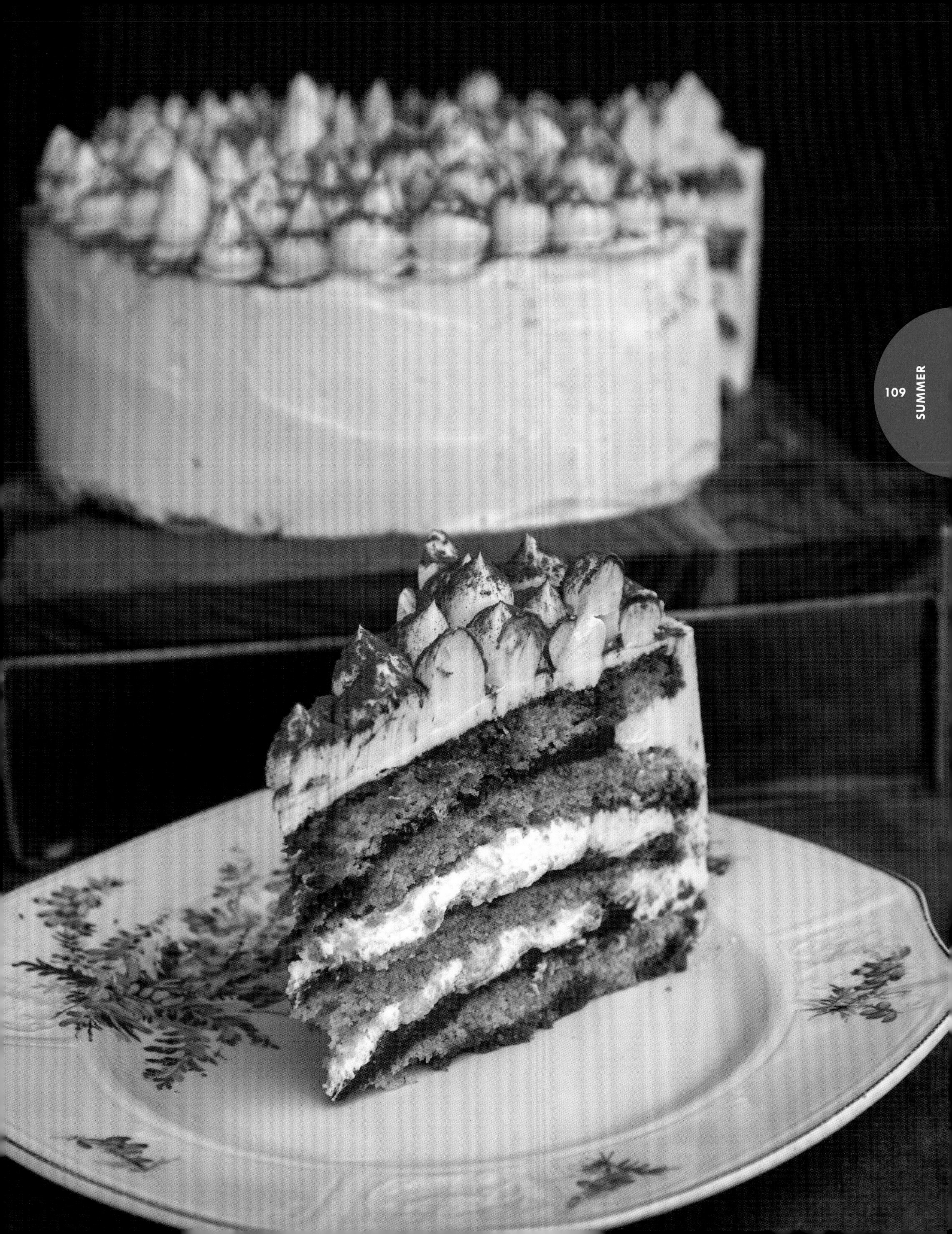

Berry Berry Good Chocolate Cake

Serves 16

DF, GF, VEGAN

This cake has been a labour of love; we wanted to create the perfect vegan chocolate cake that was moist and rich, but also gluten free. I'm very pleased to say we think we have mastered it!

CHOCOLATE CAKE

1¼ cup (125g) **GROUND ALMONDS**

2 cups (approx 260g) **PLAIN GLUTEN FREE FLOUR** – we use Bakel or Edmonds

¾ cup (75g) **COCOA POWDER**

½ cup (110g) **CASTER SUGAR**

1 cup (160g) soft **BROWN SUGAR**

1 tsp **BAKING POWDER**

2 tsp **BAKING SODA**

A pinch of **SALT**

3 tbsp **CHIA SEEDS**

150g **DARK VEGAN CHOCOLATE**, roughly chopped – at least 50% cocoa

3 tsp **INSTANT COFFEE**

1½ cups (375ml) **BOILING WATER**

1 cup (250ml) **VEGETABLE OIL**

2 tsp **VANILLA EXTRACT**

1 (approx 120g) small **BANANA**, well mashed – this helps to bind the cake

POACHED BERRIES & BERRY GANACHE

3 cups (420g) **FROZEN MIXED BERRIES**

3 tbsp **WATER**

3 tbsp soft **BROWN SUGAR**

200g **DARK VEGAN CHOCOLATE** – at least 50% cocoa

DECORATIONS

A mixture of **FRESH BERRIES**, for garnish

3 tbsp **FREEZE**-DRIED **BLUEBERRIES**, for garnish (optional)

A handful of **EDIBLE FLOWERS** (optional)

Preheat oven 170°C.

Grease and line the base and sides of a 23cm or 26cm spring-form cake tin with baking paper.

In a large bowl, sift together the ground almonds, gluten free flour, cocoa powder, caster sugar, brown sugar, baking powder, baking soda and salt. Mix until very well combined.

In small metal bowl place the chia seeds, chocolate and coffee. Pour over the freshly boiled water stirring until the chocolate is melted, then stir through the oil, vanilla and mashed banana.

Make a well in the middle of the dry mixture. Pour the warm wet mixture into the dry mixture and mix well until there are no lumps.

Pour the batter into the prepared tin and bake for approximately 1 hour or until the cake is springy to the touch and a skewer inserted into the centre comes out clean. Allow the cake to cool in the tin for 20 minutes before turning it out onto a wire rack. Cool the cake completely before icing it.

To prepare the poached berries and ganache: place the berries, water and sugar into a small saucepan, place over a low heat and cook for 10 minutes. Don't stir the berries too much or they will break apart. While the berries are cooking, finely grate (using a grater) the chocolate for the ganache into a small bowl.

Remove the poached berries from the heat and strain ½ cup of the hot berry juice into to the bowl with the grated chocolate. Set the rest of the berry compote aside to cool.

Using a fork or small whisk, stir the chocolate and berry juice together until smooth (if it doesn't melt completely you can pop it into the microwave for 10 second bursts on high until melted). Leave the ganache to cool and thicken for 5 – 10 minutes.

To assemble the cake: place the cake onto a serving platter. Spread the ganache over the top and around the sides of the cake. Decorate the top with the fresh berries and freeze-dried blueberries or some edible flowers. Place the cake in the refrigerator to firm up for at least an hour before cutting and serving.

Tip: use a hot dry knife to cut the cake. Serve with the poached berries and your favourite coconut yoghurt on the side. This cake keeps well in the refrigerator for up to a week.

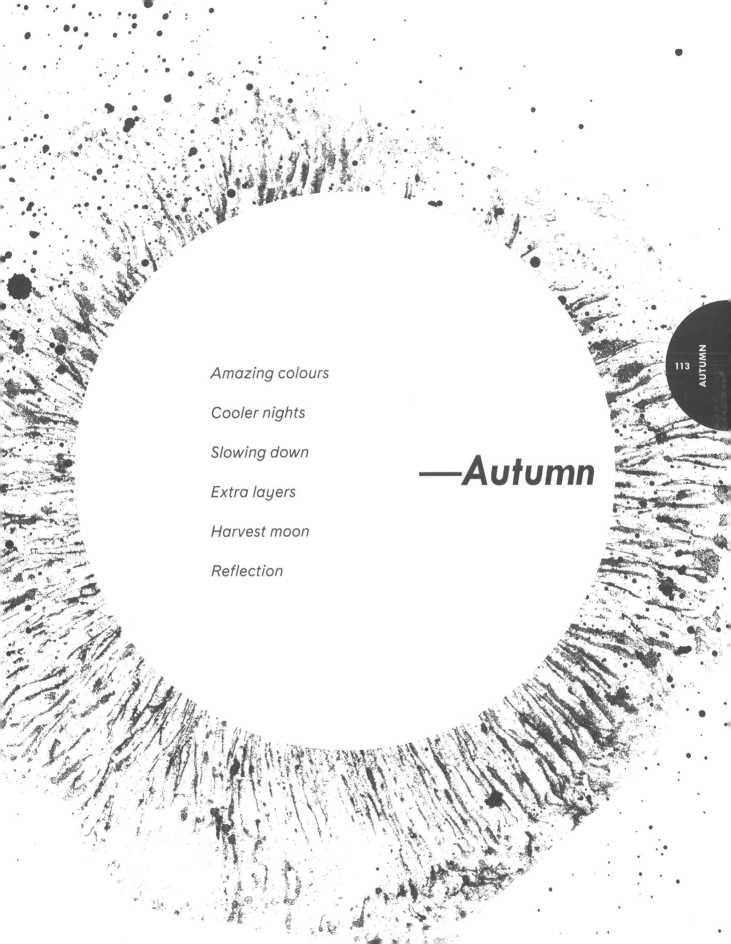

Amazing colours

Cooler nights

Slowing down

Extra layers

Harvest moon

Reflection

—*Autumn*

Crunchy Orange, Cinnamon + Cacao Granola

Serves 4

DF, VEGAN

This crunchy golden maple granola is packed full of flavour and goodness. We used a selection of walnuts, pistachio and almonds, which can easily be substituted for a selection of your favourite nuts.

GRANOLA

3 cups (300g) **QUICK COOK ROLLED OATS**
3 cups (300g) **WHOLEGRAIN OATS**
¼ cup (35g) **SUNFLOWER SEEDS**
¼ cup (40g) **PUMPKIN SEEDS**
2 tbsp **POPPY SEEDS** or **SESAME SEEDS**
1 cup (100g) **DESICCATED COCONUT**
1 cup (140g) **MIXED NUTS**, roughly chopped
1 tbsp **CACAO POWDER**
3 tsp **GROUND CINNAMON**
½ cup (125ml) melted **COCONUT OIL** or **VEGETABLE OIL**
½ cup (125ml) **MAPLE SYRUP**
ZEST and **JUICE** of 2 **ORANGES**
2 tsp **VANILLA EXTRACT**
3 tsp **FRESH GINGER**, grated
1 tsp **SALT**
5 tbsp **CACAO NIBS** (**Note:** add once the granola is cooked)

Preheat oven to 160°C.

In a large mixing bowl mix the oats, seeds, coconut, nuts, cacao powder and cinnamon together.

In another bowl combine the oil, maple syrup, orange zest, juice, vanilla, ginger and salt. Pour the wet ingredients over the dry ingredients. Mix really well to coat the grains and seeds in the oil and syrup.

Spread the granola mixture out evenly onto 2 large baking trays. Place in the oven to bake for 30 – 40 minutes or until the granola is nicely toasted. Stir the granola often to ensure it is evenly toasted.

Note: the granola will become crunchier once cold.

Remove from the oven and stir through the cacao nibs while the granola is still warm. Once cool, store in an airtight container or a large jar with a tight fitting lid.

Fruity Feijoa + Cardamom Flapjack Pancakes

Serves 4 to 6

Delightfully addictive is the best way to describe these fluffy American style pancakes. Serve them warm and drizzled in maple syrup as a weekend treat.

You can substitute the feijoa with any other seasonal fruit or berries of your choice.

PANCAKES

2¼ cup (340g) **SELF RAISING FLOUR**
3 tbsp **CASTER SUGAR**
½ tsp **SALT**
6 **CARDAMOM PODS**, seeds only, crushed (or ¼ tsp **CARDAMOM POWDER**)
1½ cups (375ml) **MILK**
ZEST of 1 **LEMON** + 4 tbsp **LEMON JUICE**
2 **EGGS**
2 tsp **VANILLA EXTRACT**
80g **BUTTER**, melted
1 cup **FEIJOA PULP**, roughly chopped
VEGETABLE OIL or **COCONUT OIL**, for frying

TO SERVE

MAPLE SYRUP
NATURAL YOGHURT

In a mixing bowl combine the flour, sugar, salt and cardamom.

In a mixing bowl mix the milk with the lemon juice and zest. Let it sit for a few minutes to allow it to curdle (this is an easy way to make buttermilk).

Whisk the egg into the curdled milk, than add the vanilla, melted butter and feijoa pulp. Stir until well combined.

Make a well in the middle of the flour mix and pour in the wet ingredients. Using a fork stir until just combined — don't over mix it. The batter should be thick and a little bit lumpy. Set aside for 5 minutes to rest.

Place a frying pan over a low to medium heat with a dash of oil. Using a ¼ cup measure pour the batter into the pan. Don't overcrowd the pan as this makes it hard to flip them.

Cook until bubbles start to form on the top of the flapjacks then flip them over to lightly brown the other side.

To serve: drizzle the flapjacks with maple syrup and natural yoghurt.

Easter Brioche Hot Cross Buns

Makes 12 hot cross buns

The tradition of making hot cross buns is ingrained in our childhood memories; little fingers kneading the dough, piping the tops with wiggly crosses, the sweet smell of spiced sticky buns fresh out of the oven.

These brioche buns are light, fluffy, buttery, sweetly spiced and delicious. This recipe is easily doubled to make a large batch of buns. We highly recommend using freshly ground cinnamon as this makes a huge difference to the flavour.

HOT CROSS BUNS

ZEST and *JUICE* of 1 large *ORANGE*
½ cup (100g) *MIXED PEEL*
¾ cup (110g) *DRIED FRUIT* — we use *CRANBERRIES*, *CURRANTS* and *RAISINS*
200g *UNSALTED BUTTER*, diced + extra for greasing the tray
1 cup (250ml) *MILK*
3½ cups (530g) *HIGH GRADE FLOUR* + extra for dusting and rolling the dough
1 tbsp *FRESHLY GROUND CINNAMON* (approx. 2 *CINNAMON QUILLS*, ground)
3 tsp *MIXED SPICE*
2 tsp *GROUND CARDAMOM*
A big pinch of *GROUND NUTMEG* and *GROUND CLOVES*
1½ tsp *SALT*
1½ tbsp *DRIED YEAST*
4 large *EGGS*, slightly beaten
¾ cup (120g) soft *BROWN SUGAR*
EGGWASH for brushing the tops of the buns

ICING FOR THE CROSSES

¼ cup (40g) *PLAIN FLOUR*
1 tbsp *ICING SUGAR*
COLD WATER

GLAZE

1 tbsp *HONEY* + 1 tsp *HOT WATER*, mixed together

To prepare the fruit: in a small saucepan mix the orange zest and juice with the mixed peel and dried fruit. Place over a low heat and gently simmer until the juice is warm. Set aside for the fruit to soak up the juice and allow to cool.

To prepare the brioche dough: melt the butter and milk together, either in the microwave or in a saucepan over a medium heat.

In a large mixing bowl combine the flour, spices and salt together. Make a well in the middle of the flour. Add the warm butter mixture, sprinkle over the yeast and leave for 5 minutes to foam up.

In another bowl whisk the eggs and sugar together. Pour the egg mixture into the foamed up yeast and stir until the batter is well combined.

Pour in the fruit and orange juice. Stir the batter vigorously using a wooden spoon for a few minutes until well combined.

Note: the dough should be quite sticky. Cover and place in a warm place to rise. You want the dough to double in size, which can take a couple of hours.

To prepare the hot cross buns: line a baking tray with baking paper. Lightly flour your bench and tip the dough out onto the flour. Using well-floured hands, lightly knead the dough for a couple of minutes. Divide the dough into 12 even portions.

Gently form each portion of dough into a ball and place on the baking trays so they are snug but still have room to rise. Cover and leave to rise in a warm spot for about 20 minutes or until they have doubled in size.

To prepare the icing for the crosses: in a small bowl combine the flour, icing sugar and water. Using a fork, whisk in enough water to form a thick paste that is a good piping consistency.

If it is too thick add more water or if too thin add a little more flour. Transfer the mix into a piping bag or a zip lock bag and cut a bottom corner off.

To bake the buns: preheat oven to 180°C.

Gently brush the tops of the buns with eggwash. Pipe crosses over the top of the buns. Place in the oven and bake for 20 – 30 minutes or until cooked through. Remove from the oven, and while the buns are still hot brush the tops with the honey glaze.

Portobello Mushrooms

Topped w/ Persian Lentils

Serves 4 to 6

DF, GF OPTION, VEGETARIAN

A delicious recipe created for us by Andrea Saunders, whom we were delighted to have back in the kitchen to help us work on our third book, as she was instrumental in the creation of our first collection, Ripe Recipes.

BAKED MUSHROOMS

1 cup (200g) **PUY LENTILS**
3 tbsp **OLIVE OIL**
1 **ONION**, peeled, finely sliced
4 cloves **GARLIC**, peeled, finely chopped
1½ tbsp **PERSIAN SPICE MIX** (see pg 239) or **MIDDLE EASTERN SPICE MIX**
1 x 400g can **DICED TOMATOES**
½ cup (20g) **FRESH CORIANDER**, roughly chopped
1 tsp **SALT**
8 – 10 large **PORTOBELLO MUSHROOMS**, stems removed
80g soft **GOAT FETA**
¼ cup (15g) **PANKO BREAD CRUMBS** (omit if gluten intolerant)

Preheat oven to 180°C.

Line a large baking tray with baking paper.

To cook the lentils: in a large saucepan add the lentils and 3 cups of water. Place over a medium heat and simmer for 20 – 25 minutes or until the lentils are tender. Remove from the heat, drain well and set aside to cool a little.

To prepare the mushrooms: place a large frying pan over a medium heat and add the olive oil. When hot add the onions and garlic and cook for a few minutes until the onions are soft.

Stir the spice mix through the onions, then add the tomatoes and simmer for a few minutes. Remove from the heat and stir through the coriander, salt and lentils.

Drizzle olive oil onto the prepared baking tray. Place the mushrooms on the tray. Spoon the lentil mix evenly on top of the mushrooms. Crumble the feta over and sprinkle with the breadcrumbs. Bake for 15 – 20 minutes until the mushrooms are cooked through.

Serve with the *MOROCCAN CARROT SALAD (see pg 136)* or *ARTICHOKE, TOMATO + PINENUT SALAD WITH ROAST OLIVE DRESSING (see pg 70)*.

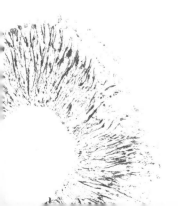

The Great Green Frittata

Makes 10 to 20

DF, GF, VEGETARIAN

This is Maggie McMillan's tasty and extremely healthy frittata loaded with greens. Basically you can use any combination of vegetables and greens for this frittata, whatever is in season or plentiful in the garden.

For those who are not sensitive to dairy try adding a handful of grated cheese or feta to the mix.

FRITTATA

8 **EGGS**
¾ cup **MILK** of your choice; nut, soy or oat milk all work well
1½ tsp **SALT**
½ tsp freshly **GROUND BLACK PEPPER**
3 **COURGETTES**, thinly sliced on an angle
½ **FENNEL BULB**, thinly sliced
1 head **BROCCOLI**, cut into bite sized florets
100g **GREEN BEANS**, topped and tailed, roughly chopped
2 tbsp **OLIVE OIL** + some for frying
SALT and freshly **GROUND BLACK PEPPER**, for seasoning the vegetables
400g **LEAFY GREENS** — we use a mix of **SPINACH**, **CAVOLO NERO** and **SILVERBEET**
1 **LEEK**, trimmed, white and green parts, finely sliced
2 tbsp **FRESH ROSEMARY**, finely chopped
1 tbsp **WHOLEGRAIN MUSTARD**
½ cup (80g) **FRESH** or **FROZEN PEAS**

Preheat oven to 180°C.

Grease a 30cm solid based pie dish or paella pan with oil.

In a bowl whisk the eggs, milk, salt and pepper together.

Set aside a few slices of courgette and fennel to decorate the top of the frittata. Place the remaining courgette and fennel, along with the broccoli and beans into a roasting dish.

Drizzle the 2 tablespoons of olive oil over the vegetables and season well with salt and freshly ground black pepper. Place in the oven to roast for 10 minutes.

Rinse all the leafy greens and drain well. Remove any tough stems and roughly chop.

Place a large frying pan over a medium heat and add a good splash of olive oil. Add the leeks and rosemary. Cook for a few minutes until soft but still vibrant.

Stir through the mustard and cook for a few seconds. Add the leafy greens and stir through until lightly wilted, then remove from the heat and add the peas.

Mix all the vegetables together and place into the pie tin or paella pan. Pour the egg mix over and using a fork or your fingers, lift the vegetables so that the egg mix is evenly distributed.

Place the reserved slices of courgette and fennel on the top. Bake for 40 — 50 minutes or until the egg mix is cooked through.

Note: if the top starts to brown too quickly cover with a piece of baking paper. Remove from the oven and leave to cool in the tin for 10 minutes before cutting.

French Green Lentil Soup

Serves 6 to 8

DF, GF, VEGAN

A classic hearty vegetable soup, best served with a good book and snuggly slippers, beside a warm fire. This is a very adaptable recipe. You can use any root vegetables you have on hand.

SOUP

2 tbsp **OLIVE OIL**
1 **ONION**, peeled, diced
2 **CARROTS**, peeled, diced
2 **CELERY STALKS**, diced
1 **LEEK**, trimmed, green and white part diced
2 **SWEDES** or **PARSNIPS**, peeled, diced
3 cloves **GARLIC**, peeled, crushed and roughly chopped
1½ tbsp **FRESH THYME**, roughly chopped (or 2 tsp **DRIED THYME**)
1 lt **VEGETABLE STOCK**
1½ lt **WATER**
1 cup (200g) **FRENCH PUY LENTILS** or **BROWN LENTILS**
2 **BAY LEAVES**
2 tsp **SALT**
½ tsp freshly **GROUND BLACK PEPPER**
2 cups (120g) **KALE** or **CAVOLO NERO**, roughly chopped
½ cup (20g) **FRESH CURLY PARSLEY**, finely chopped

Place a large stockpot over a medium heat; add the olive oil, onion, carrot, celery, leek, swede or parsnip, garlic and thyme. Cook for 5 minutes stirring often.

Add the stock, water, lentils, bay leaves, salt and pepper. Increase the heat to high and bring to a boil. Once boiling reduce the heat to a gentle simmer for 25 – 30 minutes or until the lentils are cooked through.

Stir in the kale or cavolo nero and parsley. Adjust the seasoning if needed. Serve with a good wholesome loaf of bread — try *GRANDAVE'S SEEDY BREAD (see pg 128).*

Nourishing Turmeric, Carrot, Lime + Coconut Soup

Serves 4 to 6

DF, GF, VEGAN

This soup is loaded with all the good stuff to help prevent colds and sniffles.

SOUP

3 *tbsp* **COCONUT OIL**

1 **ONION**, *peeled, roughly chopped*

4 *cloves* **GARLIC**, *peeled, crushed and roughly chopped*

2 *tbsp* **FRESH GINGER**, *grated*

1 – 2 **FRESH RED CHILLIES**, *finely chopped (or 1 tsp of dried)*

2 *tsp* **FRESH TURMERIC**, *grated (or 1 tsp turmeric powder)*

6 **KAFFIR LIME LEAVES**, *roughly chopped*

6 **CARROTS**, *peeled, roughly chopped*

2 **SWEDES**, *peeled, roughly chopped*

1 *tbsp* **COCONUT SUGAR** *or* **RAW SUGAR**

1 *tsp* **SALT**

1 *lt* **VEGETABLE STOCK**

2 *cups (500ml)* **WATER**

JUICE *of 1* **LIME**

1 *cup (250ml)* **COCONUT CREAM**

Place a large stockpot over a medium heat; add the coconut oil, onion, garlic, ginger, chilli, turmeric and kaffir lime leaves. Fry for a few minutes stirring often. Add the carrot, swede, coconut sugar, salt, vegetable stock and water.

Cook for 30 minutes or until the vegetables are tender and cooked through. Remove from the heat. Stir through the lime juice and using a stick blender, blend until smooth. Stir through the coconut cream and season to taste.

Grandave's Seedy Bread

Makes 2 loaves

DF, VEGAN

Grandave is Amy Melchior's grandfather and she has very fond memories of summer holidays spent with him on Waiheke Island making this bread and eating it with fresh tomatoes and basil from her granny's garden.

These loaves are so tasty and easy to make, you will never want to buy bread again.

Here's to keeping Grandave's great bread legacy alive. Thanks for sharing Amy.

YEAST MIX

300ml **WARM WATER**
2 tbsp **DRY YEAST**
1 tsp **RAW SUGAR**
1 tsp **PLAIN FLOUR**

THE BREAD

3 cups (450g) **WHOLEMEAL FLOUR**
3 cups (450g) **PLAIN FLOUR**
¼ cup (60g) **SESAME SEEDS**
½ cup (70g) **SUNFLOWER SEEDS**
½ cup (75g) **PUMPKIN SEEDS** (reserve 2 tbsp for the topping)
2 tbsp **LSA MIX**
2 tbsp **GROUND FLAX SEED**
2½ tsp **SALT**
650ml **WATER**
2 tbsp **BLACKSTRAP MOLASSES**
3 tbsp **OLIVE OIL**

Preheat oven to 200°C.

Grease and line two 12 x 22cm loaf tins with baking paper.

To prepare the yeast mix: place the warm water into a small bowl, sprinkle over the yeast, sugar and flour. Leave to foam up.

To prepare the bread: in a large mixing bowl combine all the dry ingredients. Make a well in the middle of the flour.

In a measuring jug mix the water, molasses and olive oil together.

Pour the wet mix and the yeast mixture into the well in the flour. Using a wooden spoon mix until the bread dough is well combined. The dough will be like a wet sticky batter.

Divide the dough evenly between the 2 loaf tins. Sprinkle the top of the loaves with the reserved pumpkin seeds and a pinch of salt.

Leave the loaves to rise in a warm place for 15 – 20 minutes, or until they have doubled in size.

Place the loaves into the hot oven to bake for 10 minutes, then reduce the heat to 180°C and bake for 40 – 45 minutes.

Check if the loaves are cooked through by tapping the top of the loaves. If they sound hollow they are ready.

Remove from the oven and leave in the tin for a few minutes before turning out to cool on a wire rack.

Yum Yum Sushi Salad

w/

Hot Smoked Salmon

Serves 4 to 6

DF, GF

A delicious brown rice salad loaded with goodness and the umami flavours of Japan.

This salad is a hearty meal in its own right and you will be happy if there are any leftovers, as this is a great salad for work or school lunch boxes.

SALAD

1½ cups (300g) **BROWN SHORT GRAIN RICE** or **SUSHI RICE**
1½ cups (225g) shelled **EDAMAME BEANS**
½ head **BROCCOLI**, finely chopped
2 cups (120g) **CAVOLO NERO** or **KALE**, finely chopped
½ **TELEGRAPH CUCUMBER**, diced
2 tbsp **SESAME SEEDS**, toasted
1 ripe **AVOCADO**, skin and stone removed, diced
1 cup (60g) **MUNG BEAN SPROUTS**, roughly chopped
2 **SPRING ONIONS**, green and white part finely sliced
2 tbsp **PICKLED PINK GINGER**, finely chopped
200g **HOT-SMOKED SALMON** or **FRESH BAKED SALMON**
(for cooking instructions (see pg 232)

JAPANESE DRESSING

2 tbsp **GLUTEN FREE TAMARI SOY SAUCE**
3 tbsp **LIME JUICE**
2 tbsp **RICE WINE VINEGAR**
2 tbsp **MIRIN**
1 tbsp soft **BROWN SUGAR** or **HONEY**
¼ tsp **SALT**

GARNISH

JAPANESE MAYO or **SESAME MAYO** (see pg 245)
4 – 6 tbsp **JAPANESE SEAWEED SPRINKLE – FURIKAKE** (see pg 240)
3 small packets **TOASTED SEASONED SEAWEED** or 4 sheets of **NORI**, lightly toasted

To prepare the rice: in a large saucepan, add the rice and 6 cups of warm water. Place over a medium-high heat and cover with a lid. Cook for 20 – 25 minutes until the rice is cooked through. Drain through a sieve and set aside to cool a little.

To prepare the dressing: whisk all the ingredients together in a small bowl.

To prepare the salad: lightly blanch the edamame beans and broccoli for a few minutes in a pot of boiling water placed over a high heat. Drain and refresh under cold running water.

In a large serving bowl add the rice, edamame beans, broccoli, cavolo nero, cucumber, sesame seeds, avocado, mung beans, spring onion and pickled ginger.

To serve: pour the dressing over the salad and mix until well combined. Flake the salmon through the salad and toss to combine.

Divide the salad into individual bowls, top with Japanese mayo or sesame mayo and seaweed sprinkle. Crumble the toasted seaweed over the top.

Rock the Casbah

—

Harissa Roasted Chickpea + Pumpkin Salad

Serves 4 to 6

GF, VEGETARIAN

This salad makes a delicious meal served with grilled fish, chicken or haloumi with a side of toasted pita chips.

SALAD

2 tbsp **OLIVE OIL**

800g **PUMPKIN** *or* **WINTER SQUASH** *skin on, cut into large bite size pieces*

3 **CARROTS** *skin on, cut into bite size pieces*

1 **RED ONION**, *peeled, sliced into chunky wedges*

1 x 400g can **CHICKPEAS**, *rinsed and drained*

2 tsp **CUMIN SEEDS**

2 tsp **FENNEL SEEDS**

2 tsp **SALT**

¼ cup **RED HARISSA** *(see pg 249)*

1 cup (60g) **SPINACH**, *roughly chopped*

1 cup (40g) **FRESH CORIANDER**, *roughly chopped*

1 cup (40g) **FRESH ITALIAN PARSLEY**, *finely chopped*

¼ cup (40g) **GOLDEN RAISINS**

HARISSA YOGHURT DRESSING

½ cup (125ml) **NATURAL YOGHURT**

A pinch of **SALT**

2 – 3 tbsp **RED HARISSA** *(see pg 249)*

Preheat oven to 200°C.

Line two baking trays with baking paper.

To prepare the salad: in a large mixing bowl combine the olive oil, pumpkin, carrot, red onion, chickpeas, spices, salt and the Red Harissa. Mix the vegetables in the spices until well coated.

Transfer onto the prepared trays. Cook for 20 – 25 minutes until well roasted and crispy. Remove from the oven and set aside to cool a little.

To prepare the harissa yoghurt dressing: in a small bowl mix the yoghurt and salt together. Lightly stir through the Red Harissa.

To serve: transfer the roasted vegetables and chickpeas onto a serving platter. Mix through the spinach, coriander, parsley and golden raisins. Drizzle over some of the dressing. Serve the remainder on the side.

Mary's Roast Parsnip + Fig Salad

Serves 4 to 6

DF, VEGAN

We have truly been blessed having Mary Cox, otherwise known as "Mother Mary" cooking in our kitchen. The salads she creates are inspiring, beautiful and truly delicious.

FIG AND ORANGE CIDER DRESSING

1 cup (190g) **FRESH** or **DRIED FIGS**, *diced*
ZEST *and* **JUICE** *of 2* **ORANGES**
4 tbsp **OLIVE OIL**
4 tbsp **CIDER VINEGAR**
A pinch of **SALT** and freshly **GROUND BLACK PEPPER**

SALAD

1 cup (200g) **FINE BULGUR WHEAT**
1 cup (250ml) **BOILING WATER**
6 **PARSNIPS**, *skin on, cut into bite size pieces*
2 tbsp **OLIVE OIL**
½ tsp **TURMERIC POWDER**
½ tsp **SALT** and freshly **GROUND BLACK PEPPER**
1 cup (120g) **WALNUTS**
1 cup (40g) **FRESH CURLY PARSLEY**, *finely chopped*
2 **SPRING ONIONS**, *white and the green part, finely sliced*
¼ cup (40g) **BARBERRIES** or **CRANBERRIES**

Preheat oven to 180°C.

Line a baking tray with baking paper.

To prepare the dressing: in a small bowl combine the figs, orange zest and juice, olive oil and cider vinegar.

Stir through the salt and pepper and set aside to allow the figs to plump up.

To prepare the salad: in a small bowl add the bulgur wheat, pour over 1 cup of boiling water and cover with a plate.

Set aside for 15 minutes to allow the bulgur wheat to swell.

Place the parsnips on the prepared baking tray and drizzle over the olive oil. Sprinkle over the turmeric, salt and pepper.

Turn the parsnips to coat in the turmeric and oil. Place in the oven to roast for 15 minutes.

Add the walnuts to the tray and cook for a further 5 – 10 minutes or until the parsnips are cooked through and the walnuts are lightly toasted.

Remove from the oven and set aside to cool.

To serve: place all the ingredients in a large serving bowl. Mix until well combined. Adjust the seasoning if needed.

Moroccan Carrot Salad

Serves 6 to 8

GF, DF, VEGAN

A wonderful salad that is very tasty and so easy to make. We think this is the new Ripe Raw Energy.

If you can't find preserved lemons, use the zest of 2 lemons.

This is a great dressing to have on hand as it will transform any salad into a delightful taste sensation.

SALAD

8 – 10 **CARROTS**, peeled and grated (approximately 4 cups of grated carrot)
2 cups (120g) **CAVOLO NERO** or **SPINACH**, stem removed, leaves finely sliced
¾ cup (100g) **DRIED DATES**, roughly chopped
½ cup (20g) **FRESH MINT**, finely sliced
½ cup (20g) **FRESH ITALIAN PARSLEY**, roughly chopped
A good pinch of **SALT**
3 – 4 tbsp **DUKKAH** (see pg 241)

MOROCCAN DRESSING

1 clove **GARLIC**, peeled, finely chopped
4 tsp **DIJON MUSTARD**
4 tbsp **MAPLE SYRUP** or **COCONUT SUGAR**
2 tsp **CUMIN SEEDS**, toasted
1 tsp **SUMAC**
1 **PRESERVED LEMON**, skin only (flesh discarded) very finely diced
5 tbsp **CIDER VINEGAR**
4 tbsp **EXTRA VIRGIN OLIVE OIL**

In a large serving bowl place all the ingredients for the salad except the dukkah and mix well.

To prepare the dressing: in a small bowl whisk together the ingredients until well combined.

To serve: pour the dressing over the salad and mix until well combined. Sprinkle the dukkah over the top just before serving.

Crunchy Quinoa Salad

w/

Maple Pecans

Serves 4 to 6

GF, DF, VEGAN

A modern twist on the classic Waldorf salad. This simple, wholesome and slightly healthier version is loaded with greens and the goodness of quinoa, topped with delicious maple caramelised pecans and good old granny smith apples.

SALAD

1 cup (200g) **QUINOA**
1 tbsp **OLIVE OIL**
2 **GRANNY SMITH APPLES**, *skin on, core removed, roughly diced*
½ cup (60g) **PECANS**
2 tbsp **MAPLE SYRUP**
2 **CELERY STALKS**, *finely sliced*
6 **GHERKINS**, *diced*
2 cups (120g) **SILVERBEET** or **SPINACH LEAVES**, *finely chopped*
1 cup (40g) **ROCKET**, *roughly chopped*
½ cup (20g) **FRESH ITALIAN PARSLEY**, *roughly chopped*

MAPLE AND RED WINE VINAIGRETTE

2 tbsp **OLIVE OIL**
2 tbsp **MAPLE SYRUP**
2 tbsp **RED WINE VINEGAR**
1 tsp **DIJON MUSTARD**
½ tsp **SALT** and freshly **GROUND BLACK PEPPER**

To prepare the quinoa: in a large saucepan add the quinoa and 3 cups of hot water. Place over a high heat and bring to the boil.

Reduce the heat and cover with a lid. Cook for 15 minutes, drain through a sieve and set aside to cool.

To prepare the caramelised apples and pecans: place a frying pan over a medium heat and add the oil. When hot add the apples, pecans and maple syrup.

Cook for a few minutes until caramelised. Remove from the heat and transfer into a small bowl. Set aside to cool.

To prepare the dressing: place all the ingredients into a jar and whisk until well combined.

To serve: place the quinoa, celery, gherkin, silverbeet, rocket and parsley in a large serving bowl. Pour over the dressing and mix until well combined. Top with the caramelised apples and pecans.

Roasted Broccoli + Pinenut Salad

Serves 4 to 6

DF, GF, VEGAN

A classic Ripe Deli salad that is simple to make. Serve with roast lamb, chicken or baked salmon.

SALAD

2 heads **BROCCOLI**, *cut into small florets and the tender half of the stem thinly sliced*
½ cup (80g) **PUMPKIN SEEDS**
2 tbsp **PINENUTS**
2 tsp **FRESH OREGANO** (or 1 tsp **DRIED OREGANO**)
2 tbsp **OLIVE OIL**
½ tsp **SALT** and freshly **GROUND BLACK PEPPER**
1 cup (40g) **FRESH ITALIAN PARSLEY**
2 cups (120g) **BABY SPINACH**
¼ cup (40g) **DRIED SOUR CHERRIES** or **CRANBERRIES**, *roughly chopped*

RED WINE DRESSING

2½ tbsp **RED WINE VINEGAR**
2 tbsp **EXTRA VIRGIN OLIVE OIL**
1 clove **GARLIC**, *peeled and finely chopped*
2 tsp **DIJON MUSTARD**
2 tsp **MAPLE SYRUP** or soft **BROWN SUGAR**

Preheat oven to 180°C.

Line a baking tray with baking paper.

To prepare the salad: in a mixing bowl combine the broccoli, pumpkin seeds, pinenuts, oregano, olive oil, salt and pepper.

Toss to coat the broccoli in the oil. Place on the baking tray in an even layer.

Roast for 15 — 20 minutes, until the broccoli is tender and the seeds are toasted. Remove from the oven and set aside to cool.

To prepare the dressing: in a small jar, whisk all the ingredients together.

To serve: transfer the roasted broccoli, seeds and nuts into a serving bowl. Add the parsley, baby spinach and sour cherries or cranberries. Pour the dressing over the salad and toss to combine.

Black Bean, Mushroom + Kale Burger Patties

Makes 12 patties

DF, GF, VEGAN

Delicious lightly spiced vegan burger patties loaded with wholesome goodness. These beauties may even convince meat eaters that eating beans and kale ain't that bad!

BLACK BEAN PATTIES

2 tbsp **OLIVE OIL**

1 **RED ONION**, peeled, finely diced

4 cloves **GARLIC**, peeled, crushed and finely chopped

4 **FLAT MUSHROOMS**, roughly diced

8 **BUTTON MUSHROOMS**, roughly diced

2 **CHIPOTLE CHILLIES** in **ADOBO SAUCE**, finely chopped + 1 tbsp of sauce

1 tsp **GROUND CUMIN**

1 tsp **GROUND CORIANDER**

2 tsp **SMOKED PAPRIKA**

2 tsp **SALT**

2 cups (120g) **KALE**, stems removed, finely chopped

2 tbsp **PEANUT BUTTER**

2 tbsp **CHIA SEEDS**

1 tsp **BALSAMIC VINEGAR**

4 tbsp **TOMATO SAUCE** or **TOMATO PUREE**

¾ cup (100g) **FINE POLENTA**

1 x 400g can **BLACK BEANS**, rinsed and drained

To prepare the patty mix: place a frying pan over a medium heat and add the oil. When hot add the onion, garlic and mushrooms.

Cook for a few minutes, stirring often. Add the chillies, spices and salt. Cook for a minute and then stir through the kale until it is wilted.

Remove from the heat and transfer into a large mixing bowl. Add all the remaining ingredients. Using a fork, mash the black beans into the mix. Stir until well combined.

Cover the mix and place in the refrigerator for 30 minutes to cool and firm. Remove from the refrigerator and shape in to 12 patties.

Note: if you don't want to cook them all, these vegetarian patties freeze well.

Place a frying pan over a medium heat with a splash of oil. Cook for a few minutes on each side or until lightly browned and heated through.

To serve: place in a toasted burger bun with your favourite fillings and chutney or try a bunless burger by wrapping the patties in fresh crunchy iceberg leaves. Serve with our *FIERY AFRICAN TOMATO SAUCE (see pg 248)* or *RED HARISSA (see pg 249)*.

Crispy Coconut Lime Fish Bites

Serves 4

DF

Bring the flavours of South East Asia to the table with these tasty little fish bites.

FISH BITES

800g firm **WHITE FISH FILLETS**
2 **KAFFIR LIME LEAVES**, *very finely chopped*
ZEST *and* **JUICE** *of 2* **LIMES**
2 tsp **COCONUT SUGAR**
¾ cup (120g) **PLAIN FLOUR**
1 tsp **SALT** *and freshly* **GROUND BLACK PEPPER**
1 cup (250ml) **COCONUT MILK**
1 **EGG**
1 cup (100g) **DESICCATED COCONUT**
1 cup (60g) **PANKO CRUMBS**
1 cup (250ml) **VEGETABLE OIL** *for frying*

To prepare the fish: cut the fish into bite size pieces. Place in a bowl with the kaffir lime leaves, lime zest, juice and coconut sugar. Turn to coat in the lime juice and leave to marinate for 10 minutes.

On a large plate combine the flour, salt and pepper. In a bowl whisk together the coconut milk and egg.

On a second plate mix the desiccated coconut and panko crumbs together until well combined.

Lightly coat the fish pieces in the flour and then dip them into the coconut milk and egg mix. Next roll the fish bites in the desiccated coconut and panko crumbs.

To cook the fish: place a wok or a large frying pan over a medium high heat. Add the oil. When hot add some of the fish bites. Cook the fish in batches so as not to overcrowd the pan.

Fry for a few minutes on each side. Drain on paper towels and season with salt and freshly ground black pepper. Serve with the Spicy *SRIRACHA MAYO (see pg 18)* and *BANGKOK BABY SALAD (see pg 80).*

Peruvian Roast Chicken

w/

Chipotle Mayo

Serves 4

GF, DF

This is our new go to roast chicken recipe, it's delicioso! It's mild enough for kids and non-chilli eaters. If you like it hot add a few more Chipotle chillies to the marinade.

ROAST CHICKEN

1 **WHOLE CHICKEN** (size 16)
2 **LEMONS**
2 **LIMES**
1 cup (250ml) **CHICKEN STOCK** or **WATER**
3 **BAY LEAVES**

PERUVIAN MARINADE

1 – 2 tbsp **CHIPOTLE CHILLIES** in **ADOBO SAUCE** (a few chillies + sauce), finely chopped
1½ tbsp **RED WINE VINEGAR**
1 tbsp soft **BROWN SUGAR**
4 tbsp **OLIVE OIL**
4 cloves **GARLIC**, peeled, crushed and finely chopped
1 tbsp **GROUND CUMIN**
1 tbsp **SMOKED PAPRIKA**
2 tsp **FRESH OREGANO**, roughly chopped (or 1 tsp of **DRIED OREGANO**)
2 tsp **SALT**
½ tsp freshly **GROUND BLACK PEPPER**

CHIPOTLE LIME MAYO

1 – 2 tbsp **CHIPOTLE CHILLIES** in **ADOBO SAUCE** (a few chillies sauce), finely chopped
ZEST and **JUICE** of 1 **LIME**
2 tsp **HONEY**
½ cup good quality **MAYONNAISE**
2 tbsp **FRESH CORIANDER** or **FRESH PARSLEY**, finely chopped

Spatchcock the chicken by placing the chicken on a chopping board, breast side down. Cut along the length of the backbone. Turn the chicken breast side up, and splay open.

To prepare the Peruvian marinade: in a small bowl, combine the chipotle chilli, red wine vinegar, sugar, olive oil, garlic, cumin, paprika, oregano, salt and pepper. Add the zest and juice of 1 lemon.

To prepare the chipotle lime mayo: mix all the ingredients together in a small bowl.

Preheat oven to 180°C.

To cook the chicken: place the chicken in a deep-sided roasting dish. Squeeze the juice of ½ the second lemon over the chicken. Rub the marinade all over the chicken.

Slice the remaining ½ a lemon and the limes into quarters. Place them under and around the chicken; pop a quarter of a lime under each wing. Add the chicken stock or water and the bay leaves to the baking dish.

Roast for 1 hour or until the chicken is cooked through. After 40 minutes, baste the chicken every now and then with the juices from the bottom of the roasting dish.

To serve: place the roast chicken on a serving platter with the chipotle mayo on the side. Serve with the *STICKY MANGO* and *AVOCADO SLAW (see pg 72)*.

Ziva's Beef Cheeks

Serves 6 to 8

DF, GF

Ziva Radlovaki created this recipe for our take home night meals, which proved to be hugely popular. The long, slow cooking of the beef cheeks is what gives this dish its melt in your mouth feel and its delicious richness.

BEEF CHEEKS

2kg (4 cheeks) **BEEF CHEEKS**
SALT and freshly **GROUND BLACK PEPPER**, to season the beef
2 tbsp **OLIVE OIL**
2 **RED ONIONS**, peeled, finely chopped
3 cloves **GARLIC**, peeled, finely chopped
2 tsp **GROUND CUMIN**
2 tsp **GROUND CORIANDER**
3 cups (750ml) good quality **BEEF STOCK**
1 cup (250ml) **WATER**
3 tbsp **POMEGRANATE MOLASSES**
2 tbsp **FRESH LEMON JUICE**
2 tbsp soft **BROWN SUGAR**

Preheat oven to 160°C.

To prepare the beef cheeks: cut the beef cheeks in half and trim off any sinew or fat. Season the beef with a little salt and lots of freshly ground black pepper.

To cook the beef cheeks: place a flameproof casserole dish over a high heat and add the olive oil.

When hot add beef cheeks. Cook for a few minutes on each side until well browned. Remove the cheeks and set aside in a bowl.

Add the onions and garlic to the casserole dish. Cook for a few minutes until the onions are translucent.

Stir in the cumin, coriander, salt and pepper. Add the stock, water, pomegranate molasses, lemon juice, sugar and the beef cheeks.

Bring to a gentle simmer, then cover with a tight fitting lid and place in the oven. Cook for 3½ hours or until the meat is extremely tender and falling apart.

Remove from the oven and adjust seasoning to taste. Ziva serves this dish with homemade potato gnocchi or creamy polenta.

Persian Slow Roasted Lamb

Serves 8

GF, DF

Moreish and divine is the best way to describe this slow cooked lamb. The exotic scents that fill the kitchen while cooking this dish are incredible.

ROAST LAMB

2 – 2.5kg Leg of **LAMB**, bone in
¼ cup (60ml) **OLIVE OIL**
2 whole **GARLIC BULBS**, cloves separated, peeled and lightly smashed
½ tsp **SALT**
¼ cup (60g) **PERSIAN SPICE MIX** (see pg 239) + 2 tbsp extra
2 **ONIONS**, peeled, cut into wedges
1 **LEMON**, cut into wedges, pips removed
1½ cups (375ml) **WATER**

To prepare the lamb: lightly score the fat on the lamb. Cut plenty of small deep slits into the lamb for the garlic cloves to fit into.

Place the lamb into a large roasting dish. Drizzle the olive oil over the lamb and stuff the garlic cloves into the slits.

Rub the salt and spice mix all over the lamb, pushing some of it into the slits. Cover and leave to marinate in the refrigerator for at least 2 hours or overnight.

To cook the lamb: preheat oven to 160°C.

Place the onions and lemon under the lamb. Add the water and the extra 2 tbsp of spice mix to the roasting pan.

Cover tightly with foil, place onto the lowest shelf of the oven and cook for 3 ½ hours.

Baste the lamb with the juices from the bottom of the pan occasionally.

Top up the water if needed. There should be approximately 1 cup of liquid in the bottom of the pan while the lamb is roasting.

After 3 ½ hours of cooking increase the heat to 180°C, remove the foil and roast for a further 20 minutes or until the fat has become crispy. The meat should now easily fall away from the bone.

Remove from the oven. Use a fork to shred the meat into the juices in the bottom of the pan and season to taste.

Serve with *POMEGRANATE GLAZED CARROTS AND KUMARA (see pg 222)* or the *MOROCCAN CARROT SALAD (see pg 136)* with toasted pita and *FETA WHIP (see pg 180).*

Ripe's Melting Moments

Chai Spiced or Passionfruit

Makes 15

EGG FREE

Melting moments are a firm favourite at Ripe. Lynn Colbert, our wonderful head baker, has lost count of how many millions of these delicious, melt in your mouth biscuits she has made over the years at Ripe Deli.

CHAI SPICED MELTING MOMENTS

1 cup (150g) **PLAIN FLOUR**
1 cup (150g) **CORNFLOUR**
½ tsp **BAKING POWDER**
½ tsp **MIXED SPICE**
¼ tsp **GROUND CARDAMOM**
½ tsp **GROUND CINNAMON**
½ tsp **GROUND GINGER**
200g **UNSALTED BUTTER**, softened
¾ cup (100g) **ICING SUGAR**
1 tsp **VANILLA EXTRACT**

Preheat oven to 160°C.

Grease and line two baking trays with baking paper.

To prepare chai spiced melting moments: in a mixing bowl sift together the flour, cornflour, baking powder and all the spices. Using a cake mixer fitted with a balloon whisk, cream together the butter, icing sugar and vanilla until creamy and pale.

Add the dry ingredients to the creamed butter. Using a spatula, mix until well combined. Scoop heaped teaspoons of the mixture and roll into 30 small balls. Place on the prepared trays. Press the tops with the palm of your hand or a fork to flatten them a little.

Place in the oven to bake for 10 – 12 minutes or until just starting to firm up – watch they don't brown. Remove from the oven and set aside to cool completely before icing them.

Note: they will become firmer as they cool.

CHAI ICING

80g **UNSALTED BUTTER**, softened
1 ½ cups (230g) **ICING SUGAR**
1 tsp **VANILLA EXTRACT**
¼ tsp **MIXED SPICE**
¼ tsp **GROUND CARDAMOM**
¼ tsp **GROUND CINNAMON**
¼ tsp **GROUND GINGER**

To prepare the chai icing: beat the butter, icing sugar and vanilla together. Add the spices and mix in 3 tsp warm water. Beat until light and creamy.

Spread some of the icing over one of the biscuits and sandwich it together with another biscuit. Repeat this until all the biscuits have been filled. Store in an airtight container.

PASSIONFRUIT MELTING MOMENTS

To prepare passionfruit melting moments: replace all the spices in the dry ingredients with 2 tbsp freeze-dried passionfruit powder. Follow the method for making the biscuits in the recipe for *CHAI SPICED MELTING MOMENTS*.

To prepare passionfruit icing: replace the Chai spices and the 3 tsp of water with 3 tbsp Passionfruit pulp (approximately 3 fresh fruit). Follow the method for making the icing in the recipe above.

Dark Chocolate Spiced Anzac Biscuits

Makes approximately 20 biscuits

DF

Anzac biscuits are a traditional kiwi biscuit. We've added rich dark chocolate and sweetly scented spices to tickle your taste buds.

We tested a few different versions of this biscuit, but this recipe was the winner, as every time we made a batch the biscuits were all gone as soon as they were out of the oven.

BISCUITS

1 cup (150g) **PLAIN FLOUR**
1½ cups (150g) **QUICK COOK ROLLED OATS**
½ cup (50g) **DESICCATED COCONUT**
¾ cup (120g) soft **BROWN SUGAR**
A pinch of **SALT**
½ tsp **GROUND CINNAMON**
½ tsp **GROUND CARDAMOM**
½ tsp **GROUND GINGER**
½ tsp **GROUND ALLSPICE**
¼ cup (60ml) **WARM WATER**
1 tsp **BAKING SODA**
160g **UNSALTED BUTTER**, roughly diced
1½ tbsp **BLACKSTRAP MOLASSES** or **TREACLE**
1 tsp **VANILLA EXTRACT**
100g good quality **DARK CHOCOLATE**
   (we use Whittaker's Dark Ghana), finely chopped

Preheat oven to 180°C.

Line 2 baking trays with baking paper.

In a large mixing bowl add the flour, oats, coconut, brown sugar, salt and all the spices. Mix until well combined. In a small bowl mix the warm water and baking soda together.

In a saucepan add the diced butter, molasses and vanilla. Place over a medium heat and melt together, stirring constantly. Remove from the heat and pour the baking soda mixture into the hot butter; stir well.

Note: the baking soda will react with the hot butter mixture and foam up so have your dry mix close at hand.

Pour the wet mix into the dry mix and stir well to combine. Let the mixture cool for a minute before stirring through the dark chocolate.

Roll the mixture into walnut sized balls. Place onto the prepared trays and flatten them well with the palm of your hand. Make sure there is enough space for them to spread during cooking.

Bake for 10 – 12 minutes. Remove from the oven and allow to cool for a few minutes on the tray before transferring them to a wire rack to cool completely. Store in an airtight container.

Alison's Feijoa Lime Coconut Loaf

w/

Lime Glaze

Makes 2 loaves

A great recipe from my friend Alison Worth, a chef turned scientist and planet saver. These feijoa loaves are totally moist and delicious without the glaze, but if you want to take it to the next level add the glaze!

FEIJOA LOAF

1½ cups (370g) **FEIJOA PULP** (8 to 10 feijoas), roughly chopped
1½ cups (120g) **LONG THREAD COCONUT** (**DESICCATED COCONUT** works well too)
ZEST of 2 **LIMES**
JUICE of 3 **LIMES**
185g **UNSALTED BUTTER**, softened
1¼ cups (280g) **CASTER SUGAR**
3 **EGGS**
2¼ cups (340g) **SELF RAISING FLOUR**
1½ tsp **BAKING SODA**
A pinch of **SALT**
1¼ cup (310ml) **UNSWEETENED YOGHURT**

THE GLAZE

½ cup (75g) **ICING SUGAR**
JUICE and **ZEST** of 1 **LIME**

Preheat oven to 180°C.

Grease and line two 12 x 22cm loaf tins with baking paper.

In a medium sized mixing bowl combine the feijoa pulp, coconut, lime zest and juice. Set aside for 10 minutes to allow the coconut to soak up the juices.

Using an handheld electric beater or cake mixer beat the butter and sugar together until light and creamy. Add the eggs one at a time, beating well and scraping down the inside of the bowl after each addition.

Sift the flour, baking soda and salt on top of the creamed mixture, but do not fold it in yet. Then add the yoghurt and feijoa mixture and fold it all together until just combined (it will fizz up a bit – I love the science!).

Divide the mix evenly between loaf tins and bake for 40 – 45 minutes or until a skewer inserted into the centre comes out clean. Remove from the oven. Set aside in the tins to cool for 10 minutes before turning out onto a wire rack.

To prepare the glaze: mix all the ingredients together and pour over the warm loaves.

These loaves are delicious served with natural yoghurt.

Note: these loaves freeze well (unglazed). When feijoas are not in season try substituting them with banana, peach or apricots.

Salted Caramel + Dark Chocolate Brownie

Serves 12

GF

We have merged two of our famously decadent slices together to produce this bombshell. **THE RICHIE (see pg 48)** *and* **ROCKO** *(from our first cookbook). Plus it's gluten free, which makes a whole lot more of our customers extremely happy. Watch out, it is totally addictive.*

SALTED CARAMEL FILLING

1 x 395g can **SWEETENED CONDENSED MILK**
80g **UNSALTED BUTTER**, *diced*
3 tbsp **GOLDEN SYRUP**
1½ tsp **FLAKY SEA SALT**

BROWNIE

300g **UNSALTED BUTTER**, *diced*
300g **DARK CHOCOLATE**, *minimum 50% cocoa, chopped*
6 large **EGGS**
1⅓ cups (300g) **CASTER SUGAR**
1 tsp **VANILLA EXTRACT**
1 cup (150g) **PLAIN GLUTEN FREE FLOUR** *(we use Edmonds or Bakels)*
1 cup (100g) **COCOA POWDER**

Preheat oven to 180°C.

Grease and line a 20 x 30cm high-sided slice tin, making sure that there is plenty of baking paper up the sides of the tin as this brownie rises up quite a lot.

To prepare the caramel: in a saucepan over a low to medium heat combine the condensed milk, butter and golden syrup. Stir constantly with a wooden spoon as this mixture catches easily. Stir for 2 — 3 minutes until the mixture has thickened. Remove from the heat and stir through the salt. Set aside to cool a little.

To prepare the brownie: melt the butter and chocolate together. Do this either in a heatproof bowl over a saucepan of simmering water on a medium low heat, or use your microwave on a high heat, in short bursts of 30 seconds for a minute or so, until just melted. Stir with a fork until combined and set aside to cool a little.

In a large mixing bowl using a whisk or handheld electric beater, whisk the eggs, sugar and vanilla together until thick. Add the warm melted chocolate mixture and mix until smooth and glossy.

In a small bowl combine the flour and cocoa powder. Sift the dry mix over the wet mixture. Using a large metal spoon fold the dry ingredients into the wet mixture until just combined. Don't over mix it otherwise it will make the brownie tough.

To assemble the brownie: pour half the brownie mixture into the slice tin. Using a large spoon dollop spoonfuls of the caramel mixture onto the brownie. Carefully spread the caramel out until it covers the brownie.

Drizzle the remaining brownie mixture over the top. Carefully spread the brownie mixture so it covers the caramel layer. If this is too fiddly you can just marble brownie mixture through the caramel.

Place in the oven to bake for 45 — 55 minutes until a glossy crust has formed and the brownie is just set. Remove from the oven and allow to cool in the tin for at least an hour before cutting.

Note: placing the brownie in the refrigerator for half an hour makes cutting it even easier. This brownie keeps well if stored in an airtight container.

Tamarillo + Cinnamon Almond Polenta Cake

Serves 12

GF

Amy Melchior created this moist, light, gluten free cake. When tamarillos are out of season, stone fruit or tart berries such as blackberries or cherries make a lovely substitute.

TAMARILLO CAKE

220g **UNSALTED BUTTER**, softened
1 cup (220g) **CASTER SUGAR**
2 tsp **VANILLA EXTRACT**
3 **EGGS**
ZEST and **JUICE** of 3 large **MANDARINS** or 1 **ORANGE**
2 cups (200g) **GROUND ALMONDS**
1 cup (140g) **FINE POLENTA**
1½ tsp **CINNAMON**
1½ tsp **BAKING POWDER**
5 **TAMARILLOS**, halved and flesh scooped out
¼ cup (20g) **FLAKED NATURAL ALMONDS**
1 tbsp **MAPLE SYRUP** or **HONEY**
ICING SUGAR for dusting

Preheat oven to 160°C.

Grease a 30cm fluted tart tin and line the base with baking paper.

Using an handheld electric beater or cake mixer, cream the butter, sugar and vanilla together until light and fluffy.

Beat the eggs, one at a time, into the creamed mixture, scraping down the inside of the bowl after each addition. Add the zest and juice of the mandarins or orange. Blend until well combined — it will curdle a bit but that's fine.

In a small bowl combine the ground almonds, polenta, cinnamon and baking powder. Add the almond mixture to the creamed mixture. Beat until well combined.

Spread the mixture into the tin. Place the tamarillos on top. Don't press the tamarillos down into the mixture otherwise the cake will rise up and cover them. Sprinkle over the flaked almonds. Bake for 40 — 45 minutes.

Remove from the oven and leave to cool for 10 minutes before removing the tart from the tin. Drizzle the maple syrup or honey over the tamarillos and dust with a little icing sugar. Best served warm with natural yoghurt.

Warm fires

Comfort food

Snowy mountains

Hibernation

Woolly jumpers

Winter chills

Hot toddies

—Winter

Broccoli + Spinach Cheesy Scones

Makes 8 large scones

VEGETARIAN

These are super easy and versatile scones; swap the broccoli for cauliflower or grated courgettes. In the summer use a couple of diced fresh tomatoes instead of sundried.

SCONES

1½ cups (160g) **BROCCOLI**, *cut into large florets*
2¼ cups (340g) **PLAIN FLOUR**
1¼ tsp **SALT**
½ tsp **BAKING SODA**
1½ tsp **BAKING POWDER**
1 tsp **CUMIN SEEDS**
100g **UNSALTED BUTTER**, *cold, grated*
1 **EGG**
½ cup (125ml) **NATURAL YOGHURT**
½ cup (125ml) **MILK**
1 cup (40g) **SPINACH LEAVES**, *roughly chopped*
1 **SPRING ONION**, *green and white parts, finely chopped*
10 (65g) **SUNDRIED TOMATOES**, *roughly chopped*
½ cup (50g) **CHEDDAR CHEESE**, *grated*

Preheat oven to 200°C.

To blanch the broccoli: half fill a saucepan with hot water. Bring to the boil over a high heat. Add the broccoli and cook for 2 minutes. Drain and refresh under cold running water. Finely chop the broccoli and set aside.

To prepare the scones: in a large mixing bowl combine the flour, salt, baking soda, baking powder and cumin. Add the cold grated butter and using your fingertips, rub it into the dry mix until it resembles fine breadcrumbs.

In a small bowl lightly whisk the egg, yoghurt and milk together.

Make a well in the middle of the flour mix. Add the egg mixture along with the broccoli, spinach, spring onion, sundried tomatoes and cheese. Mix until just combined.

Transfer the dough onto a lightly floured baking tray. Pat the dough into a rectangle that is approximately 2cm high and cut into 8 triangles.

Separate the scones out a little so they have room to rise. Brush the tops with a little milk and bake for 12 – 15 minutes or until cooked through.

Good to Go Overnight Oats

Makes 2 x 1lt jars

DF, VEGAN

A quick go-to nutritional breakfast. Amaranth is a powerful little seed that punches above its weight in nutritional goodness. LSA is a mix of ground linseed, sunflower seeds and almonds. Some mixes now also include other nutritional seeds and nuts – the more the better, we say!

FRUITY WHOLEGRAIN OATS

4 cups (400g) **NATURAL WHOLEGRAIN OATS**
½ cup **AMARANTH**, toasted or puffed
¼ cup (30g) **LSA**
2 tbsp **CHIA SEEDS**
1 tsp **GROUND CINNAMON**
1½ cup (105g) **LONG THREAD COCONUT**
¼ cup (30g) **HAZELNUTS**, sliced
¼ cup (25g) **NATURAL SLICED ALMONDS**
3 cups (300g) **DRIED FRUIT**, diced (we use **FIGS**, **PRUNES**, **APRICOTS** and **CRANBERRIES**)

SEEDY NUTTY WHOLEGRAIN OATS

4 cups (400g) **NATURAL WHOLEGRAIN OATS**
½ cup **AMARANTH**, toasted or puffed
¼ cup (30g) **LSA**
2 tbsp **CHIA SEEDS**
1 tsp **GROUND CINNAMON**
¼ cup (30g) **SESAME SEEDS**
½ cup (75g) **PUMPKIN SEEDS**
½ cup (60g) **SUNFLOWER SEEDS**
½ cup (60g) **PECANS** or **WALNUTS**, roughly chopped
½ cup (40g) **BANANA CHIPS**, roughly chopped
½ cup (70g) **RAISINS** or **CRANBERRIES**

To prepare each mix: place all the ingredients in a large mixing bowl. Mix until well combined. Store in large sealed jars in the refrigerator; LSA can go rancid if stored in the cupboard.

Per serve: soak ½ a cup of the mix with ½ a cup of water, apple juice or your choice of milk. Place in the refrigerator to soak overnight.

To serve: you can enjoy overnight oats straight from the refrigerator or gently warmed. Top with fresh or poached fruit, maple syrup and natural yoghurt.

Indian Spiced Cauliflower + Lentil Sausage Rolls

Makes 20 sausage rolls

VEGETARIAN, VEGAN OPTION

These lightly spiced vegetarian sausage rolls make a great addition to the lunch box. For a vegan option omit the cheese and use a vegan pastry. These sausage rolls freeze well and can be cooked from frozen, just increase the baking time by approximately 10 minutes.

LENTIL SAUSAGE ROLLS

1 cup (200g) **SPLIT RED LENTILS**
¼ cup (60ml) **VEGETABLE OIL**
1 **ONION**, peeled, finely diced
¼ (200g) **CAULIFLOWER**, finely chopped
2 cloves **GARLIC**, peeled, crushed and finely chopped
1 tbsp **FRESH GINGER**, grated
1 tbsp **GROUND CUMIN**
1 tbsp **MILD CURRY POWDER** + extra for garnish
2 tsp **PAPRIKA**
¼ cup (35g) **ROASTED SALTED CASHEW NUTS**, ground or finely chopped
1 **KUMARA**, peeled, grated
1 cup (60g) **SPINACH** or **KALE**, finely chopped
1 tbsp **SWEET SOY SAUCE**
2 tsp **SALT**
½ tsp freshly **GROUND BLACK PEPPER**
½ cup (50g) **TASTY CHEESE**, grated
4 sheets **VEGETARIAN PASTRY**

To prepare the sausage rolls: fill a saucepan with 3 cups of water and add the lentils. Place over a high heat and cook for 15 – 20 minutes or until the lentils are very soft. Drain through a sieve and set aside to cool.

Place a large frying pan over a low heat and add 2 tablespoons of the oil. When hot add the onion, cauliflower, garlic and ginger. Fry for 5 minutes stirring often. Add the rest of the oil with all the spices and stir to combine.

Add the lentils, cashew nuts, grated kumara, spinach, soy sauce, salt and pepper. Cook for a few minutes, stirring until well combined. Transfer the mixture into a bowl and place in the refrigerator to cool completely. Once cool stir through the cheese.

Defrost the pastry sheets and evenly divide the mixture between them. Roll into logs, firmly pinching the join together with your fingers and rolling it under. Lightly brush the join and the top of the pastry with eggwash (use oil if vegan).

Slice each log into 5 pieces and sprinkle the tops with a pinch of curry powder. Place in the freezer to firm up for at least 20 minutes.

To cook the sausage rolls: preheat oven to 200°C.

Place the sausage rolls onto a lined baking tray and bake for 30 minutes, or until the pastry is golden and the filling is heated through. Serve with your favourite chutney.

Pumpkin, Ricotta, Herb + Pinenut Pie

Serves 12

VEGETARIAN

A delightfully easy pie. In the summer months replace the pumpkin with courgettes.

PUMPKIN PIE

2 tbsp **OLIVE OIL**

2 **ONIONS**, peeled, finely diced

1½ tbsp **DRIED OREGANO**

4 cloves **GARLIC**, peeled, crushed and finely chopped

2 tsp **SALT**

½ tsp freshly **GROUND BLACK PEPPER**

4 large **EGGS**

250g **RICOTTA**

200g **FETA**, crumbled

800g **PUMPKIN**, peeled, grated (you want about 4½ cups)

½ cup (20g) **FRESH CURLY PARSLEY**, finely chopped

50g **BUTTER**

1 packet (375g) **FILO PASTRY**

½ cup (20g) **BREADCRUMBS**

¼ cup (40g) **PINENUTS**

¼ cup (40g) **PUMPKIN SEEDS**

Preheat oven to 180°C.

Place a large frying pan over a medium heat and add the olive oil. When hot add the onions, oregano, garlic, salt and pepper. Fry for a few minutes until the onions are translucent. Remove from the heat and set aside to cool.

In a large mixing bowl whisk the eggs, ricotta and feta together. Add the pumpkin, parsley and onion mixture. Mix until well combined.

Melt the butter and lightly grease a 30cm fluted tart tin. Lightly butter 3 sheets of filo. Place one on top of the other. Repeat this process 3 more times, so that you end up with 4 stacks of filo sheets.

Lay the filo sheets into the tart tin so the base and sides are covered with filo. You want to end up with some of the filo hanging over the edge.

Sprinkle the breadcrumbs over the base and add the pumpkin mixture. Sprinkle the top with the pinenuts and pumpkin seeds. Fold up the sides of the filo so it covers some of the pie.

Bake for 45 – 50 minutes, until the pie is cooked through and the filo is golden. Remove from the oven and allow to cool before cutting.

Amy's Dhal Fry

—

Red Lentil Dhal Tadka

Serves 4 to 6

DF, GF, VEGAN

Amy Melchior brings the delicious aroma of Indian street food into Ripe with this much-loved dhal.

It is a great quick meal that is very cheap to make and tastes delicious. Using a fresh good quality curry powder makes a big difference and gives dhal a lovely depth of flavour. Most Indian supermarkets will have their own special blend of fresh curry powder. You should find fresh curry leaves there as well; any unused curry leaves can be stored in the freezer for future use.

RED LENTIL DHAL

2 tbsp **COCONUT OIL**
1 **ONION**, peeled, diced
1 tbsp **GINGER**, grated
3 cloves **GARLIC**, peeled, crushed and finely chopped
1 tbsp good quality **CURRY POWDER** – we use **MADRAS CURRY POWDER**
½ tsp **TURMERIC POWDER**
2 cups (400g) **SPLIT RED LENTILS**
8 cups (2 lt) **WATER**
2 tsp **SALT**

TADKA – FRIED SPICE TOPPING

3 tbsp **COCONUT OIL**
1 **ONION**, peeled, thinly sliced
3 cloves **GARLIC**, peeled, lightly smashed (see note below)
A pinch of **SALT**
3 **RED CHILLIES DRIED** or **FRESH**, sliced in half (optional)
3 vine ripened **TOMATOES**, cut into wedges
1 tsp **CORIANDER SEEDS**
2 tsp **CUMIN SEEDS**
6 **CARDAMOM PODS**, lightly crushed in the pod
½ tsp **BLACK MUSTARD SEEDS**
8 **CURRY LEAVES**

To prepare the dhal: place a heatproof casserole dish or large pot over a medium heat. Add the oil, onion, ginger and garlic.

Fry for a few minutes until the onion has softened. Add the spices and lentils; cook for a few seconds, stirring constantly. Add the water then bring to the boil.

When boiling, reduce the heat to a gentle simmer and cook for 25 – 30 minutes or until the lentils are starting to disintegrate. Remove from the heat and stir in the salt. Cover and set aside while you make the tadka.

To prepare the tadka: lightly smash the garlic using the flat side of a knife, or in a mortar and pestle, then sprinkle the garlic with the salt.

Place a wok or frying pan over a high heat and add the oil. When hot add the onion and fry until crispy. Add the rest of the ingredients and fry, stirring often until the mustard seeds start to pop. Remove from the heat.

To serve: place the dhal into a serving bowl and pour the tadka over the top of the dhal. Serve with chapattis or roti, *CUMIN YOGHURT DIP (see pg 244)* or *INDIAN GREEN COCONUT CHUTNEY (see pg 247)*.

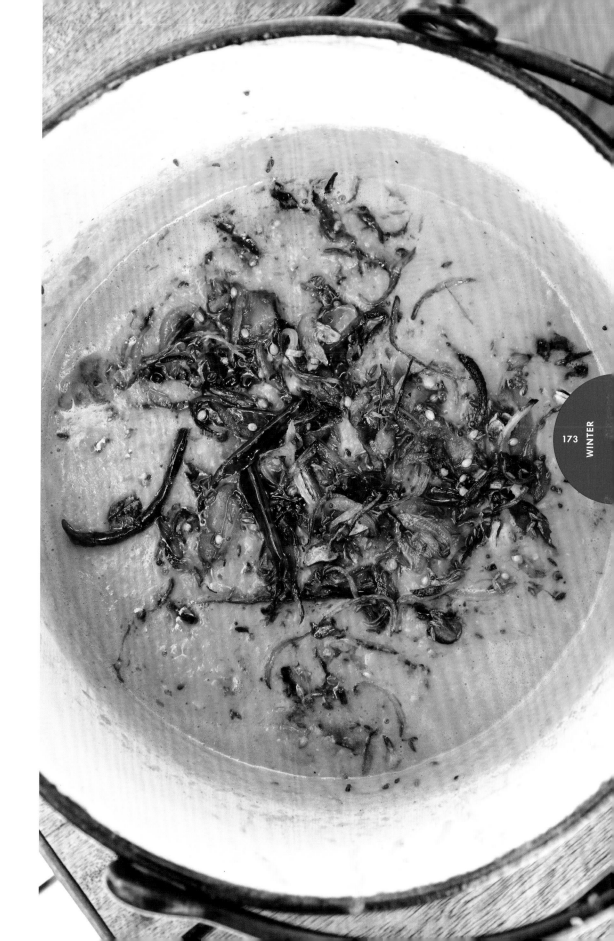

Cleansing Chicken, Leek + Silverbeet Soup

Serves 4 to 6

DF, GF

A light, nourishing soup using bone broth. Bone broth is full of nutrients that are great for your gut! To make your own bone broth, ask your butcher for 2 chicken carcasses. Pop the carcasses into a large stockpot full of water. Simmer over a low heat for a couple of hours, topping up the water as needed.

SOUP

2 tbsp **OLIVE OIL**
1 tsp **FENNEL SEEDS**
3 **CELERY STALKS**, including the tender leaves, thinly sliced
1 **LEEK**, trimmed, white and green part, diced
400g **SILVERBEET**, finely sliced including the stem
1 tbsp **FRESH TARRAGON**, finely chopped (or 1 tsp **DRIED TARRAGON**)
2 **FRESH BAY LEAVES**
2 small **CHICKEN BREASTS**, thinly sliced
2 lt **CHICKEN BONE BROTH** (or **STOCK**)
1 x 400g can **CANNELLINI** or **HARICOT BEANS**, drained
2 tsp **CIDER VINEGAR**

Place a large stockpot over a high heat. Add the oil, fennel seeds, celery, leek and the stems of the silverbeet (save the silverbeet leaves, you will add them later).

Cook for 5 minutes, stirring often. Add the tarragon, bay leaves, sliced chicken and bone broth. Bring to the boil, then reduce the heat to a gentle simmer and cook for 15 minutes.

Add the white beans, cider vinegar and silverbeet leaves. Cook for a few minutes, or until the beans are heated through. Serve with garlic croutons or *GRANDAVE'S SEEDY BREAD (see pg 128)*.

Crispy Chickpea + Cauliflower Salad

w/

Roasted Garlic Dressing

Serves 4 to 6

GF, VEGETARIAN

This salad is so tasty! It's always a challenge to get it on a plate before all the crispy chickpeas get gobbled up.

SALAD

1 **CAULIFLOWER**, florets and stem thinly sliced
3 tbsp **POMEGRANATE MOLASSES**
2 tbsp **OLIVE OIL**
½ tsp **CHILLI FLAKES**
2 tsp **GROUND CUMIN**
2 tsp **SALT**
2 x 400g cans **CHICKPEAS**, rinsed, drained and dried well
2 tsp **SMOKED PAPRIKA**
1 whole **GARLIC BULB**
1 cup (140g) **SUNFLOWER SEEDS**
½ cup (20g) **FRESH MINT**, leaves torn
½ cup (20g) **FRESH ITALIAN PARSLEY**, roughly chopped

ROASTED GARLIC DRESSING

1 cup (250ml) **NATURAL YOGHURT**
½ tsp **SALT**
1 tsp **CUMIN SEEDS**, toasted
2 tbsp **TAHINI**
ZEST and **JUICE** of 1 **LIME** or ½ **LEMON**
1 tbsp **FRESH MINT**, finely chopped

Preheat oven to 200°C.

Grease and line 2 baking trays with baking paper.

To prepare the cauliflower: place the cauliflower on to one of the baking trays. Drizzle over the pomegranate molasses and half of the olive oil. Sprinkle over the chilli, cumin and 1 teaspoon of the salt.

Roast for approximately 30 minutes, or until the cauliflower is tender and crispy around the edges. Remove from the oven and set aside to cool a little.

To prepare the chickpeas: place the chickpeas on the second baking tray and drizzle over the rest of the olive oil. Sprinkle over the paprika and the remaining salt. Give the tray a good shake to coat the chickpeas in the oil and spices.

Slice the bottom off the garlic bulb and wrap the bulb in tin foil. Place on the tray with the chickpeas and roast for 30 minutes.

Add the sunflower seeds to the tray and roast for 10 minutes longer or until the chickpeas and sunflower seeds are nice and crispy. Remove from the oven and set aside to cool a little.

To prepare the dressing: into a small bowl squeeze the roasted garlic bulb so the garlic cloves pop out and discard the skin. Add the rest of the ingredients for the dressing. Using a stick blender, blend until smooth and well combined.

To serve: place the cauliflower, chickpeas, sunflower seeds and half the fresh herbs into a large serving bowl. Drizzle half of the roasted garlic dressing over the salad and lightly toss to combine. Scatter the rest of the fresh herbs on top, and drizzle over the remaining dressing.

Cauliflower Tabouli

Serves 4 to 6

DF, GF, VEGAN

A lovely simple salad, using cauliflower instead of traditional bulgur wheat. This salad can be made in advance and left in the refrigerator to marinate in the dressing until you are ready to serve.

TABOULI SALAD

½ large **CAULIFLOWER**
1 **TELEGRAPH CUCUMBER**, *finely diced*
1 **RED ONION**, *peeled, finely diced*
1 cup (40g) **FRESH ITALIAN PARSLEY**, *roughly chopped*
1 cup (40g) **FRESH CURLY PARSLEY**, *finely chopped*
½ cup (20g) **FRESH MINT**, *roughly chopped*
2 cups (80g) **ROCKET**, *roughly chopped*
2 **SPRING ONIONS**, *white and green parts, finely sliced*

LEMON DRESSING

¼ cup (60ml) **OLIVE OIL**
¼ cup (60ml) **LEMON JUICE**
1 tsp **SUMAC**
1 tbsp **MAPLE SYRUP** or soft **BROWN SUGAR**
½ tsp **SALT** and freshly **GROUND BLACK PEPPER**

To prepare the tabouli: using a hand grater, coarsely grate the cauliflower into a large serving bowl.

You want to end up with at least 2½ cups of grated cauliflower. Add the rest of ingredients for the tabouli to the bowl and toss well to combine.

To prepare the dressing: in a small jar whisk together all the ingredients until well combined.

To serve: pour the dressing over the tabouli and toss to mix well. Season to taste with salt and freshly ground black pepper.

Spanish Roots

w/

Feta Whip

Serves 6 to 8

GF, VEGETARIAN

This hearty salad celebrates winter in all its glory by using swedes, parsnips, kumara, pumpkin, carrot and beetroot. You can use any winter vegetables that you have on hand.

If you can't find preserved lemons, you can use the zest of a fresh lemon.

SALAD

½ cup (100g) **PUY LENTILS** (French green lentils)
2 **BEETROOT** skin on, cut into thin wedges
1.5 kg mixed **WINTER VEGETABLES** (see note below) skin on, cut into chunky wedges
2 tbsp **OLIVE OIL**
3 tsp **SMOKED PAPRIKA**
2 tsp **CUMIN SEEDS**
2 tsp **FENNEL SEEDS**
1 **PRESERVED LEMON**, skin only, finely diced
1 tsp **SALT** and freshly **GROUND BLACK PEPPER**
¼ cup (35g) **SUNFLOWER SEEDS**
¼ cup (40g) **PUMPKIN SEEDS**
2 cups (120g) **CAVOLO NERO** or **KALE**, roughly chopped
½ cup (20g) **FRESH ITALIAN PARSLEY**, roughly chopped

FETA WHIP DRESSING

200g **FETA**
½ cup (125ml) **UNSWEETENED NATURAL YOGHURT**
¼ cup (60ml) **WATER**
½ tsp **CUMIN SEEDS**, toasted
1 clove **GARLIC**, peeled, crushed and finely chopped
1 tbsp **LEMON JUICE**

Note: for the 1.5kg of mixed winter vegetables listed in the ingredients, we used a combination of swedes, parsnip, kumara, pumpkin and carrot.

Preheat oven to 200°C.

Lightly oil 2 large roasting dishes.

To prepare the lentils: place a saucepan half filled with hot water over a high heat. Add the lentils, bring to the boil then reduce the heat and simmer for 15 — 20 minutes or until the lentils are tender. Remove from the heat, drain well and set aside.

To prepare the roast vegetables: place all the vegetables in a large mixing bowl. Add the olive oil, spices, preserved lemon, salt and pepper. Toss the vegetables until they are well coated in the spices and seasoning.

Place on the prepared roasting dishes and place into the oven to roast for 30 minutes.

Add the sunflower and pumpkin seeds, then roast for a further 5 — 10 minutes or until the vegetables are nicely roasted and the seeds are toasted.

To prepare the dressing: place all the ingredients into a blender and blend until smooth.

To serve: on a large serving platter, layer the vegetables with the lentils, cavolo nero and parsley.

Drizzle the dressing over as you layer. Drizzle some of the dressing over the top. Serve any remaining dressing on the side.

Anwar's Beautiful Brussels + Broccoli Salad

Serves 8

GF, VEGETARIAN

This is the perfect winter party salad, bursting with goodness and flavour. It is a big hearty salad but is easily halved to make a smaller version.

Thanks Anwar Geor for this gorgeous salad.

SALAD

600g **BRUSSELS SPROUTS**, trimmed, halved
4 tbsp **OLIVE OIL**
1 head **BROCCOLI**, cut into small florets
200g **FETA**, crumbled
SALT and freshly **GROUND BLACK PEPPER**
2 x 400g cans **CANNELLINI BEANS**, rinsed, drained well
½ cup (125g) **BASIL PESTO**
2 **CELERY STALKS**, finely sliced including the tender leaves
1 cup (40g) **FRESH ITALIAN PARSLEY**, roughly chopped
¼ cup (10g) **FRESH MINT**, leaves picked

Preheat oven to 180°C.

Grease and line 2 baking trays with baking paper.

To prepare the brussels sprouts, broccoli and feta: on one of the trays place the Brussels sprouts and drizzle over half the olive oil. Toss well to coat them in the oil.

Place the broccoli and feta on the second tray and drizzle over the remaining olive oil. Season both trays well with salt and pepper.

Place both trays in the oven to roast for 15 minutes or until the Brussels sprouts are tender and the feta is nicely roasted. Remove from the oven and set aside to cool a little.

To serve: on a large platter, mix the cannellini beans with the pesto. Add the celery and the Brussels sprouts. Toss to combine. Scatter over the broccoli, feta, parsley and mint.

Amy's Saigon Street Slaw

w/

Spicy Tofu

Serves 4 to 6

DF, GF, VEGAN

Amy Melchior created this wonderful street style slaw full of the flavours of Asia. It is a satisfying meal in its own right. Sriracha chilli sauce is a spicy and slightly tangy chilli sauce found in most supermarkets or Asian food stores.

SLAW

2 cups (400g) **EDAMAME BEANS**, shelled
2 tbsp **SESAME OIL**
1 packet (250g) **FIRM TOFU**, diced
1 – 2 tbsp **SRIRACHA CHILLI SAUCE**
2 tbsp **GLUTEN FREE TAMARI SOY SAUCE**
2 **CARROTS**, peeled, cut into match sticks or grated
1 cup (60g) **MUNG BEAN SPROUTS**
2 **SPRING ONIONS** white and green parts, finely chopped
3 cups (300g) **GREEN CABBAGE**, finely shredded
2 cups (120g) **SPINACH**, finely sliced
½ cup (20g) **FRESH CORIANDER** or **FRESH BASIL**, roughly chopped
½ cup (75g) **SALTED ROASTED PEANUTS**, finely chopped or crushed

SRIRACHA LIME DRESSING

ZEST and **JUICE** of 2 **LIMES**
4 tbsp **RICE VINEGAR**
2 – 3 tbsp **COCONUT SUGAR** or soft **BROWN SUGAR**
2 – 3 tsp **SRIRACHA CHILLI SAUCE**, more if you want it spicy
3 **KAFFIR LIME LEAVES**, finely chopped
¼ cup (60ml) **VEGETABLE OIL**
A pinch of **SALT**

To blanch the edamame beans: place a saucepan half full of water over a high heat and bring to the boil. When boiling, add the beans and cook for approximately 1 minute or until tender. Then drain and refresh under cold running water.

To prepare the tofu: place a large frying pan over a high heat and add the sesame oil. When hot add the tofu, Sriracha and soy sauce, cook for a few minutes stirring constantly. Remove from the heat and set aside to cool.

To prepare the dressing: place all the ingredients for the dressing into a small mixing bowl. Blend well using a stick blender. Adjust sweetness if needed.

To serve: in a large serving bowl combine all the ingredients for the salad including the tofu and edamame beans. Pour the dressing over the salad and toss well to combine.

Mary's Warm Shitake + Soba Noodles

w/ Chicken

Serves 4 to 6

DF, GF

Another beautiful salad created by our "Mother Mary" the salad saint Mary Cox!

GINGER MARINADE

40g **FRESH GINGER**, *peeled, very finely sliced*
1 cup (250ml) **MIRIN**
½ cup (125ml) **GLUTEN FREE TAMARI SOY SAUCE**
½ cup (125ml) **WATER**
2 cloves **GARLIC**, *peeled, thinly sliced*

SOBA SALAD

40g **DRIED SHITAKE MUSHROOMS**, *thinly sliced*
200g **GLUTEN FREE BUCKWHEAT SOBA NOODLES**
2 – 3 tbsp **SESAME OIL**, *for frying*
1 x (200g) **CHICKEN BREAST**, *sliced lengthways through the middle and thinly sliced*
300g **BOK CHOY**, *roughly chopped*
200g **CAVOLO NERO** or **KALE**, *roughly chopped*
2 **SPRING ONIONS**, *white and green part, finely sliced*
½ cup (100g) **PINK PICKLED GINGER**, *roughly chopped*

To prepare the marinade: in a small saucepan, combine all the ingredients for the marinade. Place over a very low heat and cook for 10 minutes to allow the ginger to infuse into the marinade.

Remove from the heat, strain and discard the ginger. You should end up with approximately 2 cups of marinade.

Place the shitake mushrooms into a small mixing bowl and pour 1 cup of the hot marinade over them.

To prepare the soba noodles: fill a large saucepan with hot water and bring to the boil over a high heat. Add the soba noodles and cook for 3 minutes.

Remove from the heat and drain under cold running water. Place the soba noodles into a large serving bowl and pour over ½ cup of the marinade.

Place a wok over a high heat and add the sesame oil. When hot add the chicken and stir-fry for 3 – 5 minutes or until just cooked through, then add the bok choy and cavolo nero.

Pour in the remaining marinade and cook for a minute longer. Remove from the heat and add to the soba noodles.

To serve: into the serving bowl that has the soba noodles, chicken and vegetables in it, add the spring onions, pickled ginger and the mushrooms with all of the marinade. Mix well to coat the vegetables and noodles in the marinade.

Vegan Laksa

w/
Tofu

Serves 4 to 6

DF, GF, VEGAN

Most store bought laksa paste contains shrimp paste, so we created a laksa paste for all the lovely vegans that come for our famous curry night at Ripe. You can, of course, serve this laksa with chicken, fish or prawns if you desire.

LAKSA

100g dried **FLAT RICE NOODLES** or **CELLOPHANE NOODLES**
4 tbsp **VEGETABLE OIL**
1 **ONION**, peeled, roughly chopped
3 long **ASIAN EGGPLANTS**, roughly chopped
⅔ cup **VEGAN LAKSA PASTE** (see pg 238), add more if you like it spicy
6 cups (1.5 lt) **WATER**
1 small **KUMARA**, peeled, roughly chopped
1 **CAPSICUM**, de-seeded, roughly chopped
1 packet (250g) **TOFU**, diced
2 tsp **SALT**
1 cup (250ml) **COCONUT CREAM** (we use Kara)

GARNISH

120g **MUNG BEAN SPROUTS**
½ cup (20g) **FRESH CORIANDER**, roughly chopped
SRIRACHA CHILLI SAUCE, for those who like it hotter
2 **LIMES**, quartered

A note on noodles: there are a few different types of noodle that are vegan; rice noodles and cellophane noodles (which are usually made from mung bean flour) are in most supermarkets or Asian stores.

Dried rice noodles don't need a lot of cooking. Place the rice noodles into a bowl and cover with warm water and leave to soak. Drain them just before you add them to the laksa.

Place a large saucepan or wok over a high heat and add ½ the oil. When hot add the onion and eggplant. Cook for 5 minutes stirring often.

Stir through the laksa paste and the rest of the oil. Cook for a minute, stirring constantly. Add the water, kumara and capsicum.

Bring to the boil, then reduce the heat and cook for 20 – 25 minutes or until the kumara is cooked through. Add the noodles, tofu, salt and coconut cream.

Cook for approximately 5 minutes, until the oil starts to separate and rise to the surface.

To serve: divide the laksa evenly between the individual serving bowls and top with the mung bean sprouts and coriander. Serve with Sriracha chilli sauce, lime wedges and some fried roti on the side.

Kedgeree

w/

Smoked Fish
+ Crispy Onions

Serves 4 to 6

GF

The ultimate comfort food that is so simple to make. Take a trip to your local Indian market to buy your curry powder, it will be far superior to the supermarket variety. Our favourite for this dish is Sri Lankan curry powder or if you're after some heat try Madras curry powder.

KEDGEREE

2 tbsp **GHEE** or **BUTTER**
1 **ONION**, peeled, finely diced
6 cloves **GARLIC**, peeled, lightly crushed
2 tsp **FRESH GINGER**, grated
1 tbsp good quality **CURRY POWDER**
1 tsp **TURMERIC POWDER**
3 **WHOLE CARDAMOM PODS**, lightly crushed
½ tsp **GROUND CINNAMON**
1 **FRESH BAY LEAF**
2 tsp **SALT**
2 cups **BASMATI RICE**
4 cups (1lt) **WATER**
1 cup (160g) **FRESH** or **FROZEN PEAS**
½ cup (20g) **FRESH CORIANDER**, finely chopped
500g **SMOKED FISH**, meat picked off the bone
3 **EGGS**, boiled, peeled and cut into wedges
1 cup **CUMIN YOGHURT DIP**, (see pg 244)

CRISPY ONIONS

2 tbsp **VEGETABLE OIL**
2 **ONIONS**, peeled, halved and thinly sliced
2 tbsp **CUMIN SEEDS**
½ tsp **SALT**

To prepare the kedgeree: place a large saucepan over a medium heat; add 1 tablespoon of ghee or butter. Add the diced onion and cook for a few minutes until the onion has softened and started to caramelise.

Add the rest of the ghee or butter, then the garlic, ginger, all the spices, bay leaf, salt and rice. Cook the rice for a minute, stirring constantly.

Add the water and bring to a rolling boil. Reduce the heat to very very low, cover with a tight-fitting lid and cook for 8 minutes.

Then add the peas, cover with the lid and turn off the heat. Leave the rice to sit for 10 minutes — don't lift the lid or you will release all the steam that is cooking the rice!

To prepare the crispy onions: place a frying pan over a high heat and add the oil. When the oil is hot, add the onions. Fry for 5 minutes until the onions are caramelised and crispy.

Add the cumin seeds and salt and cook for a few seconds longer. Remove from the heat and drain on a paper towel.

To serve: using a fork fluff the rice, discard the cardamom pods and bay leaf. Transfer onto a serving platter then mix through half the coriander and crispy onions. Adjust seasoning to taste.

Scatter over the smoked fish, boiled eggs, the rest of the coriander and crispy onions. Serve with some of the cumin yoghurt drizzled over the top and the rest on the side.

African Chicken + Peanut Stew

Serves 4 to 6

DF, GF

Winter comfort is the perfect way to describe this stew, warming and hearty with the option of a little heat too.

For a vegetarian or vegan version swap the chicken meat for a large eggplant roughly diced.

AFRICAN STEW

¼ cup (60ml) **PEANUT OIL** or **VEGETABLE OIL**
600g boneless and skinless **CHICKEN THIGHS**, roughly chopped
2 **ONIONS**, peeled, roughly chopped
5 cloves **GARLIC**, peeled, lightly smashed
2 tsp **PAPRIKA**
2 tsp **CUMIN SEEDS**, toasted, ground
2 tsp **CORIANDER SEEDS**, toasted, ground
2 tsp **FRESH GINGER**, finely chopped
1 tsp **CHILLI FLAKES** (optional – if you like it hot add more)
1 tbsp **FRESH THYME**, finely chopped, or 1 tsp **DRIED THYME**
1 tbsp **FRESH OREGANO**, finely chopped or 1 tsp **DRIED OREGANO**
750ml **CHICKEN STOCK** or **WATER**
5 tbsp good quality **CRUNCHY PEANUT BUTTER**
1 x 400g can **DICED TOMATOES** or 5 large **FRESH TOMATOES**, diced
500g **KUMARA** or **PUMPKIN**, peeled, roughly chopped
1 tsp **SALT** and freshly **GROUND BLACK PEPPER**

GARNISH

¼ cup (10g) **FRESH CORIANDER**, chopped
¼ cup (35g) **ROASTED SALTED PEANUTS**, roughly chopped
1 **LIME**, cut into wedges

Preheat oven to 180°C.

Place a large flameproof casserole dish over a medium heat and add the oil. When hot add the chicken, onions and garlic.

Cook for a few minutes, stirring constantly until the onions and chicken are lightly browned. Stir through the spices, chilli and herbs and cook for a few seconds.

Add the stock or water, peanut butter, tomato, kumara or pumpkin, salt and pepper. Bring to a gentle simmer and cook for 10 minutes.

Cover the casserole dish with a tight fitting lid and place in the oven to cook for 30 minutes. Remove from the oven and adjust seasoning to taste.

To serve: top with the fresh coriander and chopped peanuts. Serve with lime wedges on the side. This stew is great served with brown rice or warm chapattis.

Get Your Mojo On

—

Ripe's Slow Roasted Pulled Pork

Serves 8

GF, DF

Succulent street-style slow roasted pork – loaded with flavour that is well worth the wait.

Ask your local butcher to debone the pork and score the skin for you.

MARINADE

¼ cup (60ml) **OLIVE OIL**
5 cloves **GARLIC**, peeled, finely chopped
1 tbsp **GROUND CUMIN**
2 tbsp **CUMIN SEEDS**
2 tbsp **SMOKED PAPRIKA**
2 tsp **SALT**
2 tsp whole **BLACK PEPPERCORNS**, crushed or ground
1 tbsp **MAPLE SYRUP** or **HONEY**

RIPE'S MOJO PORK

2 – 2.5 kg **PORK SHOULDER**, deboned, skin scored
4 **ONIONS**, peeled, thinly sliced
1 whole **BULB GARLIC**, cloves separated, peeled and smashed
A handful of **FRESH OREGANO** and/or **FRESH THYME**, roughly chopped
1 – 2 **CHIPOTLE CHILLIES** in **ADOBO SAUCE** + 2 tbsp of **ADOBO SAUCE**
1 tbsp **BALSAMIC VINEGAR**
3 tbsp **MAPLE SYRUP** or **HONEY**
2 tbsp **SMOKED PAPRIKA**
1 **CINNAMON STICK**, broken in half
2 cups (500ml) **CHICKEN STOCK** or **VEGETABLE STOCK**
1 x 400g can **DICED TOMATOES**
SALT and freshly **GROUND BLACK PEPPER** for seasoning

To prepare the marinade: in a small bowl mix all the ingredients together.

To prepare the pork: rub the marinade all over the pork and place in a bowl in the refrigerator to marinate for at least a couple of hours or overnight.

To cook the pork: preheat oven to 200°C.

In a flameproof casserole dish (or large roasting tray) add the onions, garlic and herbs.

Place the chipotle chillies and adobo sauce into a small bowl. Add the balsamic vinegar, maple syrup and paprika and blend well using a stick blender (or if you don't own a stick blender finely chop the chillies and mix them together with the rest of the ingredients).

Mix the chilli mixture and cinnamon stick with the stock and diced tomatoes then pour it into the casserole dish.

Place the pork, skin side up, on top of the onions and sauce. Place in the hot oven to roast for 30 minutes, then reduce the heat to 165°C and cover with a lid or with foil.

Cook for 3 hours, or until the meat easily falls apart when pulled with a fork. When the pork is fork-tender remove and discard the fatty layer of skin and cinnamon stick.

To serve: using tongs or forks, pull the meat apart and mix it through the sauce. Adjust seasoning to taste with salt and freshly ground black pepper. Serve with brown rice and black beans, or corn tortillas, a light slaw and **CHIPOTLE MAYO (see pg 146).**

Ripe's Slow Cooked Corned Beef

Serves 4 to 6

DF, GF OPTION

A great way of serving a cheaper cut of meat and any leftovers can be used in sandwiches the next day.

Please note malt vinegar contains gluten. To make this recipe gluten free use red wine vinegar.

CORNED BEEF

2kg **CORNED BEEF**
3 **FRESH BAY LEAVES**
1 tbsp **PICKLING SPICE**
1 tbsp **JUNIPER BERRIES**
3 tbsp **BLACKSTRAP MOLASSES** or **TREACLE**
2 **ONIONS**, cut into quarters
2 **ORANGES**, halved
1 **CELERY STALK**, roughly chopped
½ cup (125ml) **MALT VINEGAR** or **RED WINE VINEGAR** (gf)

CREAMY PICKLE AND YOGHURT SAUCE

½ cup (125ml) **NATURAL YOGHURT**
½ cup (125ml) good quality **MAYONNAISE**
2 tsp **WHOLEGRAIN MUSTARD**
8 **GHERKINS**, finely chopped
2 tbsp **FRESH DILL**, finely chopped (optional)

Rinse the corned beef really well to remove the brine.

Note: for a not so salty beef you can use silverside from the butcher and brine it yourself or just cook it without brining.

Place all the ingredients into a large flameproof casserole dish or stockpot and fill with plenty of water to cover the beef. Cover with a tight fitting lid and place over a low – medium heat.

Simmer for 2½ – 3 hours. Add more hot water when needed to ensure the water is covering the beef the whole time.

Note: you can also cook this in a slow cooker overnight for 10 – 12 hours.

To prepare the creamy pickle and yoghurt sauce: place all the ingredients in a small bowl and mix until well combined.

To serve: remove the corned beef from the cooking liquid and allow to rest for 5 minutes. Place on a serving board and slice thinly.

Serve with the creamy pickle and yoghurt sauce on the side. Try it with *TURKISH PICKLES (see pg 247)* and *DREAMY CREAMY CAULIFLOWER PUREE (see pg 226)* or boiled baby potatoes with butter.

Beaver's Beef + Prune Stew

Serves 4 to 6

DF, GF OPTION

Two very popular recipes from our previous books are from my dear friend Nicole Beaver, so here is the trifecta. Really tasty, cheap to make – plus high in fibre, it's a win win.

BEEF STEW

2 tbsp **PLAIN FLOUR** *(omit if gluten intolerant)*
SALT and freshly **GROUND BLACK PEPPER** for seasoning the beef
1.5 kg **CROSS CUT BLADE STEAK**, *cut into 2.5cm cubes*
OLIVE OIL *for frying*
1 **ONION**, *peeled, finely chopped*
3 cloves **GARLIC**, *peeled, finely chopped*
1 sprig **FRESH ROSEMARY**, *left whole*
3 **ANCHOVIES**
1½ cups (375ml) **RED WINE**
3 cups (750ml) *good quality* **BEEF STOCK**
1 tbsp **GLUTEN FREE WORCESTERSHIRE SAUCE**
1 tbsp **BALSAMIC VINEGAR**
½ tsp **SALT** and freshly **GROUND BLACK PEPPER**
250g **PRUNES**

Note: Cross Cut Blade Steak is the best cut of beef to use for this stew; it has lots of marbling that breaks down during the slow cooking to create a lovely rich sauce. Most supermarkets should have it or your local butcher will.

Preheat oven to 160°C.

Place the flour into a bowl and season well with the salt and pepper. Add the beef and toss well to coat the meat in flour.

Place a large flameproof casserole dish over a low – medium heat with a splash of oil. Add the onion, garlic, rosemary and anchovies.

Cook for 5 minutes or until the onion is translucent, stirring often.

Transfer the onion mix into a large bowl. Return the casserole dish to the heat. Increase the temperature to high and add a good splash of olive oil.

When hot, add some of the beef and brown well on all sides. Cook the beef in batches so as to not overcrowd the pan.

Add the browned beef to the onions and tip any juices from the beef in as well. Repeat the process until all the beef is nicely browned.

Place the casserole dish back on the high heat. There should be lots of crunchy bits on the bottom of the pan, which adds to the flavour.

Add the wine, stock, Worcestershire sauce and vinegar. Bring to the boil then add the beef and onion mixture, the salt, pepper and prunes.

Once the stew is simmering, cover with a tight fitting lid and place in the oven. Cook for 2½ – 3 hours until the beef is very tender.

Remove the stew from the oven and adjust seasoning if needed. Serve with the *DREAMY CREAMY CAULIFLOWER PUREE (see pg 226)* or boiled new potatoes.

Kate's Mojito Cake

Serves 12 to 16

Our lovely baker Kate Emerson-Zhang created this wickedly boozy cake based on the delicious ingredients that make a mojito. What more could you want from a cake!

MOJITO SYRUP

½ cup (110g) **CASTER SUGAR**
½ cup (125ml) **WATER**
½ cup (125ml) **WHITE RUM**
¼ cup (60ml) **LIME JUICE**

CAKE

3 cups (450g) **PLAIN FLOUR**
⅓ cup + 1 tsp (50g) **CORNFLOUR**
1¼ tsp **BAKING POWDER**
¾ tsp **BAKING SODA**
¾ tsp **SALT**
260g **UNSALTED BUTTER**, softened
1½ cups + 1 heaped tbsp (350g) **CASTER SUGAR**
¼ cup (40g) soft **BROWN SUGAR**
ZEST of 4 **LIMES**
4 large **EGGS**
1½ cups (375ml) **MILK**
1 tbsp **WHITE RUM**
¼ cup (60ml) **FRESH LIME JUICE**
1 cup (40g) **FRESH MINT LEAVES**, finely chopped + extra for garnish
1 **LIME**, sliced thinly as garnish (optional)

ICING

1 cup (150g) **ICING SUGAR**
ZEST of 1 **LIME** + 1 – 2 tbsp of **JUICE**
1 tbsp **WHITE RUM**

Preheat oven 165°C.

Grease and line a 23cm or 26cm cake tin with baking paper.

To prepare the syrup: in a small saucepan combine the sugar and water. Place over a high heat and bring to the boil. Once the sugar is dissolved, remove from the heat and allow to cool slightly before adding the rum and lime juice.

To prepare the cake: in a medium sized mixing bowl, sift the flour, cornflour, baking powder, baking soda and salt together.

Using a cake mixer or a handheld electric beater, beat the butter, caster sugar, brown sugar and lime zest until light and creamy. Add the eggs one at a time, scraping down the inside of the bowl after each addition.

In a small bowl, whisk together the milk, rum and lime juice.

Add small amounts of the dry ingredients alternately with the wet mix to the creamed butter, beating after each addition. Stir the fresh mint through the cake batter and pour into the prepared tin.

Bake for 60 – 80 minutes or until a skewer comes out clean when inserted into the centre of the cake.

Note: the bigger the cake tin the less time the cake will take to cook. If the cake starts to brown on the top, cover with a piece of baking paper.

Remove the cake from the oven and allow to cool for 10 minutes, then slowly pour the syrup evenly over the top of the cake. Leave the cake in the tin to cool completely.

To prepare the icing: in a small bowl mix the icing sugar, zest and rum into a smooth paste. Add the lime juice a little at a time until the icing is still slightly thick but dribbles easily off a spoon.

To serve: remove the cake from the tin and turn out on to a serving plate. Gently spread the icing over the top. Decorate with mint leaves and lime slices. Serve with natural yoghurt or whipped cream.

Spiced Pumpkin Cheesecake

w/

Maple Roasted Pecans

Serves 12 to 14

This deliciously decadent recipe comes from the lovely Amy Gillespie who used to bake for us at Ripe.

Making this pumpkin cheesecake is a nostalgic affair for Amy. "I have fond memories of having pumpkin pie bake offs in the kitchen with my uncle, and never quite successfully winning until I made this pumpkin cheesecake. These memories, and the experience I gained, helped shape my love of cooking and baking".

SPICED PUMPKIN

1 tbsp **GROUND CINNAMON**
1 tbsp **GROUND GINGER**
½ tsp **GROUND NUTMEG**
½ tsp **GROUND CLOVES**
¼ tsp **GROUND ALLSPICE**
¼ tsp **GROUND CARDAMOM**
750g **PUMPKIN**, peeled, cut into large 6cm chunks
¼ cup (60ml) **MAPLE SYRUP**
ZEST of 1 **ORANGE**

BASE

250g **GINGERNUT BISCUITS**
85g **BUTTER**, melted

FILLING

JUICE of 1 **ORANGE**
650g **CREAM CHEESE**, softened
150g **SOUR CREAM**
1½ cups (240g) soft **BROWN SUGAR**
¼ tsp **SALT**
2 tbsp **MAPLE SYRUP**
2 tbsp **FLOUR**
3 large **EGGS**

TOPPING

2 tbsp **MAPLE SYRUP** + some for garnish
1 cup (120g) **PECANS**
⅓ cup (50g) **PUMPKIN SEEDS**

Preheat oven to 180°C.

Grease and line a 23cm or 26cm spring-form cake tin and 2 small roasting trays with baking paper.

To prepare the spiced pumpkin: in a small bowl combine all the spices. Place the pumpkin on the prepared tray and mix with the maple syrup, orange zest and half the spice mix. Cover with foil and bake for 30 – 40 minutes. Remove from the oven and set aside to cool.

To prepare the base: using a food processor, blend the biscuits until they form a fine crumb. Add the melted butter and blend again until well combined. Press the mixture firmly into the prepared tin and place in the refrigerator to set.

To prepare the filling: using a food processor, blend the spiced pumpkin and orange juice together. Add the cream cheese, sour cream, brown sugar, salt, maple syrup, flour and the remaining spice mix. Blend until the mixture is very smooth.

Add the eggs one at a time, pulsing after each addition until well combined. Pour the cheesecake filling onto the chilled base. Reduce the temperature of the oven to 160°C.

Bake in the oven for 1 hour or until just set. It should still be a little wobbly in the middle. Remove from the oven and set aside in the tin to cool for an hour, then place in the refrigerator to cool completely.

To prepare the topping: preheat oven to 180°C.

Line 2 small baking trays with baking paper. Mix maple syrup and pecans together on the prepared tray. Place the pumpkin seeds on the other tray. Cook for approximately 8 – 10 minutes, until the pumpkin seeds are toasted and pecans are caramelised.

Note: the pumpkin seeds will cook a bit quicker than the pecans.

To serve: run a warm knife around the edge of the cheesecake to release it from the tin. Place on a serving platter and top with the maple pecans and toasted pumpkin seeds. Drizzle with a little maple syrup and serve with natural yoghurt.

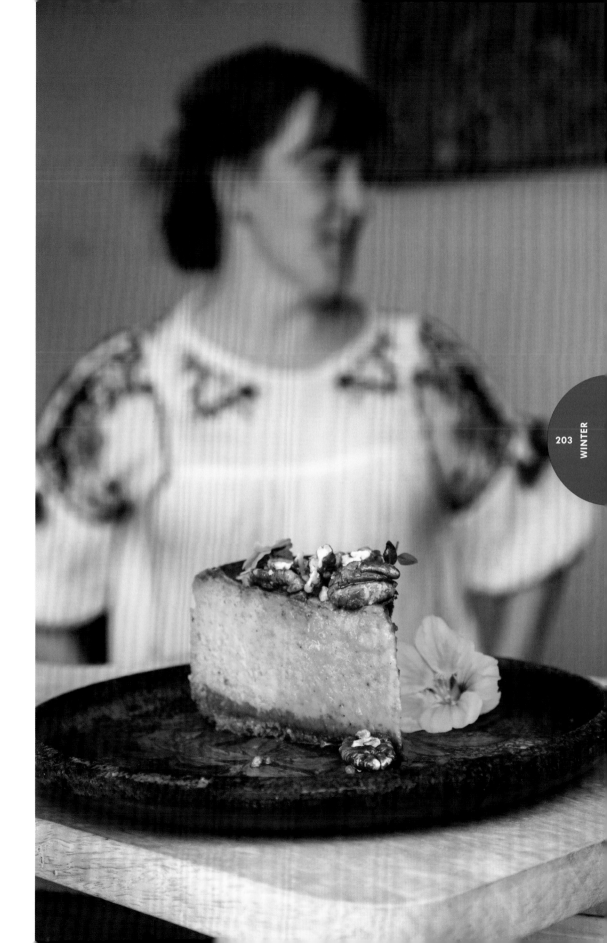

Blossoming Queenie

—

Victoria Sponge Cake

Serves 12

This cake is fit for a queen. A beautiful combination of light fluffy sponge, layered with roasted rhubarb, raspberries and Chantilly cream, delicately scented with orange blossom.

SPONGE

225g **UNSALTED BUTTER**, softened
1 cup (220g) **CASTER SUGAR**
1 tbsp **ORANGE ZEST**
4 **EGGS**
1¼ cups (190g) **SELF RAISING FLOUR**
1½ tsp **BAKING POWDER**
2½ tbsp **CORNFLOUR**
1 tsp **ORANGE BLOSSOM WATER**
4 – 6 tbsp **MILK**

CHANTILLY CREAM

300ml **FRESH CREAM**, cold
1 tbsp **ICING SUGAR**
1 tsp **ORANGE BLOSSOM WATER**
1 tsp **ORANGE ZEST**

TOPPING

4 large **RHUBARB STEMS**, sliced into
  3cm pieces
¼ cup (40g) soft **BROWN SUGAR**
1 cup (130g) frozen **RASPBERRIES**, defrosted

Preheat oven to 180°C.

Grease and line two 23cm sponge tins or spring-form cake tins and a small roasting tray with baking paper.

To prepare the sponge cakes: using a food processor, blend the butter, caster sugar, orange zest and eggs together until creamy.

In a small bowl mix together the self-raising flour, baking powder and cornflour.

Add the flour mix into the creamed mixture and lightly blend until it forms a smooth batter.

With the motor running, add the orange blossom water and enough milk achieve a smooth dropping consistency. Divide the batter evenly between the two prepared tins.

Bake for 20 – 25 minutes or until the sponges are springy to the touch and a skewer inserted into the middle comes out clean.

Remove from the oven and allow to cool in their tins for 10 minutes before turning out onto a wire rack.

To prepare the Chantilly cream: place the cream, icing sugar and orange blossom water into a metal mixing bowl.

Using an handheld electric beater or whisk, whip the cream until it is thick and holds its shape. Stir through the orange zest. Place in the refrigerator until you are ready to assemble the cake.

To prepare the topping: mix the rhubarb with the brown sugar on the prepared tray. Place in the oven to bake for 10 minutes or until soft and lightly caramelised.

Remove from the oven, transfer into a small bowl and set aside to cool. When cool, gently combine the rhubarb and raspberries.

To assemble the cake: place one of the sponges on a serving plate and spread half the cream over the top. Place the second sponge on top and spread the remaining cream over.

Top with the roasted rhubarb and raspberries before serving. This cake is best eaten as soon as it is assembled.

Thumbprint Biscuits

Makes 20

DF, VEGAN

A lovely simple recipe created by Amy Wong Kam for us way back in the early days of Ripe.

These are foolproof and fun biscuits to make with small kids.

Oat bran is full of dietary fibre and adds a lovely flavour to these biscuits. You can find oat bran and spelt flour in health food stores.

BISCUITS

1 cup (100g) **OAT BRAN**
1 cup (100g) **GROUND ALMONDS**
1 cup (125g) **PLAIN SPELT FLOUR** or **WHOLEMEAL FLOUR**
½ cup (125ml) **VEGETABLE OIL** or **COCONUT OIL**, melted
½ cup (125ml) **MAPLE SYRUP**
¼ cup (75g) good quality **BERRY** or **PLUM JAM**

Preheat oven to 180°C.

Grease and line a baking tray with baking paper.

In a large mixing bowl combine the oat bran, ground almonds and spelt flour or wholemeal flour. Pour in the oil and maple syrup and mix until well combined.

Roll into walnut sized balls and flatten them slightly. Place on the baking tray and using your thumb, push down to leave a small indentation in the middle of each biscuit. Place half a teaspoonful of jam into the indent.

Place in the oven to bake for 12 – 15 minutes. Remove from the oven and allow to cool on the tray for a few minutes before transferring onto a wire rack.

Tip: there are many options for filling for the thumbprints; try popping a strawberry or some blueberries in them, or peanut butter, banana or dark chocolate.

Spiced Pumpkin + Molasses Loaf

Makes 1 loaf

DF, VEGAN

A delicious moist and warming spiced loaf, perfect with a cuppa on a cold winter's night.

LOAF

300g **PUMPKIN**, *peeled, roughly chopped into chunks*
1½ tsp **GROUND ALLSPICE**
2 tsp **GROUND CINNAMON**
2 tsp **FRESH GINGER**, *grated*
½ tsp **SALT**
1½ tbsp **GROUND FLAX SEED** mixed with ¼ cup **HOT WATER**
½ cup (125ml) **OLIVE OIL**
¾ cup (120g) soft **BROWN SUGAR**
3 tbsp **GOLDEN SYRUP** + extra for drizzling
3 tbsp **BLACKSTRAP MOLASSES**
1½ tsp **BAKING SODA**
½ cup (125ml) **MILK** of your choice – almond, soy, oat or rice milk all work well
2 cups (300g) **WHOLEMEAL FLOUR**

Preheat oven to 180°C.

Grease and line a 12 x 22cm loaf tin with baking paper.

To prepare the pumpkin: place the pumpkin in a saucepan and fill with enough hot water to cover. Place over a high heat and cook for 10 – 15 minutes, until the pumpkin is soft. Remove from the heat and drain well.

Using a food processor, blend the pumpkin, allspice, cinnamon, ginger, salt and the flax seed mixture. Add the oil, brown sugar, golden syrup and molasses. Blend until combined.

Mix the baking soda and milk together. Pour into the blender with the pumpkin mix and blend. Add the flour and blend again until well combined. Pour into the prepared tin.

Bake for 40 – 50 minutes or until a skewer inserted into the middle comes out clean. Remove from the oven and allow to cool a little before turning out of the tin.

Drizzle a little extra golden syrup over the top before serving. Or serve as a delicious warm pudding with *VEGAN SALTED COCONUT CARAMEL SAUCE* (see pg 10) and vanilla coconut ice cream.

Lynn's Ginger Kiss Slice

Serves 10 to 12

A lovely twist on a kiwi favourite. Lynn Colbert created this light and sweetly spiced ginger kiss slice. Lynn also makes this slice with a lime and cream cheese filling which is equally as delicious.

SPONGE

1 cup (150g) **PLAIN FLOUR**
½ cup (80g) **SELF-RAISING FLOUR**
¾ tsp **BAKING SODA**
2 tsp **GROUND GINGER**
½ tsp **GROUND CARDAMOM**
  (or seeds of 6 pods, crushed)
½ cup (80g) soft **BROWN SUGAR**
100g **UNSALTED BUTTER**
¾ cup (260g) **GOLDEN SYRUP**
  + extra for drizzling
1 tbsp **ORANGE ZEST**
4cm piece of **FRESH GINGER**
2 **EGGS**
¾ cup (180ml) **MILK**

FILLING

300ml **FRESH CREAM**, *cold*
1 tsp **ORANGE ZEST**
¼ tsp **GROUND CARDAMOM**
  (or seeds of 3 pods, crushed)
¼ cup (40g) **ICING SUGAR**
  + extra for dusting

Preheat oven to 180°C.

Grease and line two 20 x 30cm slice tins with baking paper.

To prepare the sponge: in a mixing bowl sift together the flours, soda and spices. Add the brown sugar and mix until well combined.

Place the butter, golden syrup and orange zest into a small saucepan. Place over a low heat and melt together, stirring until well combined.

Remove from the heat and set aside to cool a little. Grate the ginger and using your hand squeeze the juice of the grated ginger into the butter mixture — discard the flesh.

In a small bowl, lightly whisk the eggs and milk together. Make a well in the middle of the flour mixture. Pour the butter mixture, and then the egg mixture into the flour. Stir until just combined.

Divide the batter evenly between the two slice tins. Place in the oven to bake for 10 — 12 minutes, until the sponge is springy to the touch.

Remove from the oven; allow to cool a little in the tin before turning out onto a wire rack. Cool the sponge cakes completely before filling.

To prepare the cream filling: place the cream into a metal mixing bowl. Using an handheld electric beater or whisk, beat the cream until it is just starting to thicken.

Add the orange zest, cardamom and icing sugar. Whip until the cream holds its shape.

Note: the cream filling can be refrigerated until you are ready to assemble and serve the slice.

To serve: place one of the sponge cakes onto a serving platter. Spread the cream filling evenly over the sponge. Place the second sponge cake on top.

Dust with icing sugar and drizzle over a little golden syrup when serving.

ABUNDANT VEGE

212

*Exciting recipes
that will inspire
you to get
creative with
vegetables when
nature is prolific.*

—*Abundant
Vege*

Broccoli + Iceberg Wedges w/ Blue Cheese Dressing

Serves 4 to 6

VEGETARIAN, GF

A nice quick salad with a delicious creamy dressing. This dressing also makes a great dip for crudités.

BLUE CHEESE DRESSING
¼ cup (60ml) **SOUR CREAM** or **NATURAL YOGHURT**
¼ cup (60ml) good quality **MAYONNAISE**
80g **CREAMY BLUE CHEESE**
1 clove **GARLIC**, peeled, finely chopped
2 tsp **HONEY**
2 tsp **LEMON JUICE**
2 tsp **WHOLEGRAIN MUSTARD**
1 tbsp **CIDER VINEGAR**

SALAD
½ **ICEBERG LETTUCE**, sliced into small wedges
2 **CELERY STALKS**, thinly sliced
1 head **BROCCOLI**, cut into bite sized florets
½ cup (60g) **WALNUTS**, toasted

To prepare the dressing: in a food processor (or using a stick blender), blend all the ingredients together until smooth.

If the dressing is a little thick, add a splash of water to make the dressing pourable.

Place the salad on a serving platter in layers starting with the iceberg, then celery and broccoli.

Pour the dressing over the salad then crumble the walnuts over the top.

Serve with: grilled chicken or try crunchy bacon pieces scattered over the top.

Broccoli + Buckwheat

Serves 4 to 6

VEGETARIAN, GF

1 cup **RAW BUCKWHEAT**
1 head **BROCCOLI**, cut into bite sized florets
1 cup (160g) **FROZEN PEAS**
SALT and freshly **GROUND BLACK PEPPER**
60g **BUTTER**
3 cloves **GARLIC**, peeled, crushed and finely chopped
2 sprigs of **FRESH ROSEMARY**, finely chopped

Place the buckwheat in a saucepan and cover with water. Place over a high heat and bring to the boil.

Reduce the heat and cook for approximately 15 minutes or until the buckwheat is tender and cooked through. Remove from the heat, strain through a sieve and set aside.

Refill the saucepan with hot water, place over a high heat and bring to the boil. When boiling add the broccoli and cook for a few minutes, then add the peas and cook for a minute longer.

Remove from the heat and strain. Place the buckwheat, broccoli and peas onto a serving dish; season to taste with salt and freshly ground black pepper.

Place a small saucepan over a low heat; add the butter, garlic and rosemary. Cook for a minute or so, until the garlic and rosemary has infused into the butter.

Pour over the buckwheat and mix well. Serve with shaved Parmesan and grilled chicken or salmon.

Roasted Broccolini w/ Curried Cashew Cream

Serves 4

VEGAN, GF, DF

250g **BROCCOLINI**, sliced in half lengthways
½ cup (75g) **PUMPKIN SEEDS**
2 tbsp **OLIVE OIL**
A pinch of **SALT** and freshly **GROUND BLACK PEPPER**
100g **KALE**, leaves picked

CURRIED CASHEW CREAM
½ cup (70g) **ROASTED SALTED CASHEW NUTS**
2 tsp **FRESH GINGER**, grated
1 tsp **CUMIN SEEDS**
1 tsp **GROUND CORIANDER**
A pinch **TURMERIC POWDER**
A pinch of **SALT** + freshly **GROUND BLACK PEPPER**
1 tsp **FRESH LEMON JUICE**
½ cup (125ml) **BOILING WATER**

Preheat oven to 200°C.

Place the broccolini and pumpkin seeds on a baking tray, drizzle over 1 tablespoon of the olive oil then season with the salt and pepper. Toss well to coat the broccolini and seeds in oil.

Place in the oven to roast for 15 minutes or until the broccolini is tender and the seeds are toasted. Set aside to cool a little.

To prepare the cashew cream: place all the ingredients into a jug and pour in the freshly boiled water. Set aside for 10 minutes to allow the cashews to soften. Using a stick blender, blend until smooth and creamy. The cream will thicken up as it sits; mix a little more water through if needed before serving.

To serve: place the kale in a large serving bowl or on a platter. Add the remaining olive oil and vigorously massage the oil into the kale for a few minutes. The kale will become soft and bright green. Scatter the broccolini and pumpkin seeds over the kale and drizzle some of the cashew cream over the top. Serve the remaining cashew cream on the side.

Spiced Courgettes, Beans, Peas + Coconut

Serves 4 to 6

GF, DF, VEGAN

We had quite a few requests for this recipe, which is another beauty created by the lovely Maggie McMillan.

2 tbsp **VEGETABLE OIL**
4 **COURGETTES**, diced into bite size chunks
1 tsp **TURMERIC POWDER**
1 tsp **GROUND CUMIN**
1 tsp **GROUND CORIANDER**
½ tsp **BLACK** or **YELLOW MUSTARD SEEDS**
2 tsp **GARAM MASALA**
1 tsp **SALT** and freshly **GROUND BLACK PEPPER**
3 cloves **GARLIC**, peeled, finely chopped
2cm piece of **FRESH GINGER**, grated
1 cup (70g) **LONG THREAD COCONUT**
250g **GREEN BEANS**, topped and tailed
1 cup (160g) **FRESH** or **FROZEN PEAS**

Place a large frying pan over a medium heat and add the oil. When hot add the courgettes and cook for a few minutes.

Add all the spices, salt and pepper, garlic, ginger and coconut. Fry for a minute, stirring constantly until the spices are fragrant and the coconut is lightly toasted.

Add the beans and peas along with ¼ cup of hot water. Cover the pan with a lid or metal tray to allow the beans to steam for a minute.

Remove the lid and cook for a few minutes, stirring constantly. Once the water has completely evaporated and the coconut has crisped up a bit, remove from the heat. Adjust seasoning to taste and serve.

Stacy's Vegan Calabacitas

Serves 4 to 6

VEGAN, GF, DF

Stacy Rodriguez has shared this quick and easy warm salad. It is based on a traditional Mexican dish that Stacy's family has adapted to make it vegan. It is a great warm salad, side dish or vegan taco filling. Stacy recommends cooking this dish on the barbeque to give it a lovely smoky flavour.

1½ tbsp **OLIVE OIL**
1 **ONION**, peeled, roughly diced
5 **COURGETTES**, cut into chunky bite sized pieces
2 cloves **GARLIC**, peeled, crushed and roughly chopped
2 – 3 **FRESH RED CHILLIES**, finely chopped
1 tsp **CUMIN POWDER**
3 **CORN COBS**, corn sliced off the cob
1 tsp **SALT**
1 tsp freshly **GROUND BLACK PEPPER**
¼ cup (10g) **FRESH CORIANDER**, roughly chopped
1 **LIME**, cut into wedges

Place a large frying pan over medium to high heat (or on a hot BBQ plate). Add the olive oil and the onion and cook for a few minutes until the onion is translucent.

Add the courgettes, garlic, chilli and cumin and cook for 5 minutes, then add the corn and cook for a few minutes longer or until the corn turns bright yellow.

The vegetables should still have a bit of crunch in them. Add the salt and pepper. Remove from the heat and add the coriander just before serving. Serve with wedges of lime.

Roasted Courgette w/ Zatar

Serves 4

VEGAN, DF, GF

A light and simple side dish that is loaded with flavours of the Middle East. Serve with labneh or hummus as a lovely side dish.

6 **COURGETTES**, sliced in half lengthways
2 tbsp **OLIVE OIL**
1 tbsp **SESAME SEEDS**, toasted
A pinch **SALT** and freshly **GROUND BLACK PEPPER**
A pinch of **DRIED OREGANO** and **DRIED THYME**
1½ tsp **SUMAC**
½ tsp **CUMIN POWDER**

Preheat oven to 180°C.

Place the courgettes on a roasting tray and rub the olive oil all over them. In a small bowl mix the sesame seeds, salt, pepper, oregano, thyme, sumac and cumin powder together.

Sprinkle the spice mix (zatar) on top of the courgettes and roast in the oven for 20 – 25 minutes or until cooked through.

Cucumbers w/ Roasted Nectarine + Smoky Paprika Almonds

Serves 6 to 8

VEGETARIAN, GF

A winner of a salad. Lovely looking and super easy to make, filled with summery flavours.

2 tbsp **OLIVE OIL**
2 tsp **SMOKED PAPRIKA**
2 tsp **SALT**
2 tsp **MAPLE SYRUP** or **HONEY**
1 cup (120g) **NATURAL ALMONDS**
4 **NECTARINES** cut into wedges
2 **TELEGRAPH CUCUMBERS**, peeled, seeds removed, diced into bite size pieces
2 tbsp **SHERRY VINEGAR**
¼ cup (10g) **CURLY PARSLEY**, finely chopped
½ cup (20g) **BASIL LEAVES**
20g **IBERICO** or **PECORINO CHEESE**, shaved

Preheat oven to 200°C.

Line a baking tray with baking paper.

To prepare the roast almonds and nectarines: in a small bowl mix the olive oil, paprika and salt with the maple syrup (or honey). Add the almonds. Mix until they are well coated in the spices.

Pour the spiced almonds on to the prepared baking tray and roast for 10 minutes.

Add the nectarines and give the tray a good shake so the nectarines get coated in the paprika mix, then cook for 5 minutes longer. Remove from the oven and set aside to cool a little.

To serve: mix the cucumbers, sherry vinegar and herbs in a large serving bowl.

Add the almonds, nectarines and cheese, tossing gently to combine.

Nordic Cucumber Salad

Serves 4 to 6

GF, VEGETARIAN

A super easy marinated salad with a lovely light and creamy dressing.

1 **TELEGRAPH CUCUMBER**, quartered lengthways, seeds removed and thinly sliced
½ **RED ONION**, peeled, halved and thinly sliced
1 **FENNEL BULB**, thinly sliced, then roughly chopped into small pieces including the fennel fronds
2 tbsp **WHITE BALSAMIC VINEGAR**
1 tbsp **CASTER SUGAR**
1 tbsp **FRESH LEMON JUICE**
½ cup (125g) **SOUR CREAM**

To prepare the salad: in a serving bowl mix all the ingredients together except the sour cream. Place in the refrigerator to marinate for 10 minutes then mix through the sour cream and season to taste.

Lao Spicy Cucumber Salad

Serves 4 to 6

GF, DF, VEGAN

This is a zingy Lao salad that will have you reaching for a beer. This salad is perfect served with tempeh or fish, grilled on the barbeque!

CHILLI LIME DRESSING
3 – 4 **FRESH CHILLIES**, finely chopped (seeds removed if you don't like it spicy)
1 clove **GARLIC**, crushed, finely chopped
½ tsp **SALT**
ZEST and **JUICE** of 1 **LIME**
2 tbsp **RICE WINE VINEGAR**
2 tbsp **WHITE VINEGAR**
2 tbsp **COCONUT SUGAR** or **HONEY**

LAO SALAD
2 **TELEGRAPH CUCUMBERS**, cut lengthways and thinly sliced
2 **CAPSICUMS**, de seeded, finely sliced into strips
120g **MUNG BEAN SPROUTS**
¼ cup (10g) **BASIL LEAVES (THAI BASIL** is best), leaves picked
1 tsp **POPPY SEEDS**

To prepare the dressing: in a small bowl combine all the ingredients and whisk until the sugar is dissolved.

To prepare the salad: in a serving bowl combine the cucumber and capsicums. Pour the dressing over the vegetables and mix well. Place in the refrigerator to marinate for 10 minutes.

To serve: mix through the mung bean sprouts, basil and poppy seeds, when you are ready to serve.

Ginny's Tasty Tomato Sauce

Makes approximately 3 x large 1 lt jars

VEGAN, DF, GF

This one pot wonder is a recipe the lovely Ginny Kevey shared with us.

3 tbsp **OLIVE OIL**

2 **CELERY** stems, diced

3 **CARROTS**, peeled, diced

2 **ONIONS**, halved, peeled and diced

4 cloves **GARLIC**, peeled, finely chopped

2 kg of **FRESH TOMATOES**, diced or 4 x 400g cans **DICED TOMATOES**

2 **BROCCOLI** stems (or 1 whole **BROCCOLI**), roughly chopped (optional)

1 ½ tsp **SALT**

½ tsp freshly **GROUND BLACK PEPPER**

A large handful of **FRESH HERBS**, leaves picked, we used **ROSEMARY, BASIL** and **PARSLEY**, or 3 tsp **MIXED DRIED HERBS**

2 x 420g cans **BUTTER BEANS** or **CANNELLINI BEANS**, rinsed and drained

Place a large stockpot (or flameproof casserole dish) over a high heat and add the oil. When hot add the celery, carrots, onions and garlic. Cook for 5 minutes stirring often. Add the tomatoes, broccoli stems (or broccoli), salt and pepper.

Add 5 – 6 cups of water (or if using tinned tomatoes rinse the cans by filling each can with water and pouring the water into the stockpot). Place the stockpot over a high heat and bring to the boil.

When boiling add the herbs and reduce the heat to as low as possible and gently simmer for approximately 1 ½ – 2 hours, or until the sauce has reduced down by about a third. Then stir through the butter beans and cook for a further 10 minutes or until the beans are heated through.

Remove from the heat and blend well using a stick blender. Adjust seasoning to taste. This sauce freezes well and is great to have on hand when you have hungry little mouths to feed.

Tomato + Roast Capsicum Panzanella

Serves 6 to 8

VEGAN, DF, GF

6 – 8 **CAPSICUMS**

¼ cup **OLIVE OIL** (approx)

300g **SOURDOUGH LOAF**, cut into small bite sized chunks

1 kg mixed **HEIRLOOM TOMATOES**, halved, core removed, cut into bite sized chunks

1 **RED ONION**, peeled, finely diced

5 – 6 **ANCHOVY FILLETS**, roughly chopped

125g **BOCCONCINI**, balls cut in half

1 cup (40g) **FRESH BASIL LEAVES**

DRESSING

2 tbsp **OLIVE OIL**

2 tbsp **SHERRY VINEGAR**

1 tbsp **MAPLE SYRUP**

½ tsp **SALT** and freshly **GROUND BLACK PEPPER**

Preheat oven to 200°C.

To prepare the capsicums and sourdough croutons: place the capsicums on a baking tray; rub a little olive oil all over them. On a second baking tray place the cut sourdough, drizzle with olive oil and season with salt and pepper. Place the 2 trays into the oven and roast for 20 – 30 minutes or until the capsicums are well roasted and the sourdough croutons are crispy.

Remove from the oven and place the capsicums into a plastic bag. Tie a knot in the top to stop hot air escaping. Set aside for 10 minutes to allow them to sweat; this makes peeling the capsicums much easier.

Remove the capsicums and slice them in half, removing the stem and seeds. Peel and discard the skin. Slice the capsicums into strips.

In a large serving bowl combine the roasted capsicums, tomatoes and onion with the anchovies. In a small bowl whisk together all the ingredients for the dressing. Pour the dressing over the salad and mix until well combined. Mix through the croutons, bocconcini and basil leaves when you are ready to serve.

Delightfully Delicious Slow Roasted Tomatoes

Serves 4 to 6

VEGAN, GF, DF

A light and simple side dish that is loaded with the great summery flavours of sweet tomatoes.
Eat them as they are or pile them up on brushetta topped with basil.

1kg **TOMATOES**, we used a mixture of vine and cherry tomatoes

1 tbsp **SHERRY VINEGAR**

1 tbsp **POMEGRANATE MOLASSES**

2 tsp **OLIVE OIL**

1 tbsp **COCONUT SUGAR** or **MAPLE SYRUP**

2 tsp **SUMAC**

A pinch of **SALT** and freshly **GROUND BLACK PEPPER**

Preheat oven to 180°C.

Place the tomatoes into a roasting dish. Mix the rest of the ingredients together in a small bowl.

Pour the mixture over the tomatoes and place in the oven to roast for 30 minutes. When nicely roasted, remove from the oven and serve.

Pomegranate Glazed Carrots + Kumara

Serves 6 to 8

VEGAN, DF, GF

2 tsp **SUMAC**

2 tsp **CUMIN SEEDS**

½ tsp **SALT**

1 tbsp **POMEGRANATE MOLASSES** + extra for garnish

2 tbsp **MAPLE SYRUP**

3 tbsp **OLIVE OIL**

6 **CARROTS**, skin on, sliced in half lengthways, cut into large wedges

3 **ORANGE KUMARA**, skin on, chopped into large wedges

2 **RED ONIONS**, peeled and cut into large wedges

3 tbsp **POMEGRANATE SEEDS**

Preheat oven to 200°C.

Line 2 large baking trays with baking paper.

In a large mixing bowl combine the spices, salt, pomegranate molasses, maple syrup and olive oil. Add the vegetables and turn to coat in the glaze.

Place the vegetables onto the prepared trays. Roast for 30 – 35 minutes or until nicely roasted and cooked through.

To serve: place the roast vegetables on to a serving platter, drizzle over a little pomegranate molasses and sprinkle with pomegranate seeds. Serve with the *PERSIAN SLOW ROASTED LAMB (see pg 150)*.

Harissa Spiced Carrot Puree

Serves 4 to 6

VEGAN, GF, DF

Serve as a side dish with meats or fish – or with pitas as a healthy vegan dip.

8 **CARROTS**, peeled, roughly chopped

3 tbsp **OLIVE OIL** + extra for garnish

3 cloves **GARLIC**, peeled, finely chopped

2 tsp **CUMIN SEEDS**

4 tbsp **RED HARISSA PASTE** (see pg 249)

1 tbsp **LEMON JUICE**

1 tsp **SALT**

2 tbsp **DUKKAH** (see pg 241)

Place the carrots in a large saucepan and fill with enough water to cover. Place over a medium heat and cover with a lid. Cook for 20 – 25 minutes, until the carrots are very soft. Remove from the heat and drain well.

Place a frying pan over a medium heat. Add the olive oil, garlic and cumin seeds. Stirring constantly, fry for 1 – 2 minutes until the seeds are toasted.

Remove from the heat and transfer into a food processor. Add the carrots, harissa, lemon juice and salt. Blend until very smooth and well combined.

To serve: place in a serving bowl. Sprinkle over the dukkah and drizzle with a little olive oil.

Parmesan Roasted Baby Carrots

Serves 4 to 6

GF, VEGETARIAN

2 bunches **BABY CARROTS**, cleaned and tops trimmed

2 tbsp **OLIVE OIL**

2 tsp **PAPRIKA**

1 tbsp **BALSAMIC VINEGAR**

1 tbsp **HONEY** or **MAPLE SYRUP**

¼ cup (25g) **PARMESAN GRATED**

2 tbsp **FRESH ITALIAN PARSLEY**, chopped

SALT and freshly **GROUND BLACK PEPPER**

Preheat oven to 180°C.

Line a large baking tray with baking paper.

In a mixing bowl combine the carrots with the olive oil, paprika, balsamic and honey. Toss until well coated. Place the carrots onto the prepared baking tray.

Place in the oven to roast for 25 – 30 minutes or until tender and nicely roasted.

Remove from the oven and sprinkle the Parmesan over the carrots. Return the tray to the oven for a few minutes or until the Parmesan is melted and golden.

To serve: transfer onto a serving platter, scatter over the parsley and season to taste.

Autumn Green Slaw w/ Toasted Seeds

Serves 4

GF, VEGETARIAN

400g **CELERIAC**
JUICE of ½ **LEMON** mixed with ¼ cup **COLD WATER**
2 tbsp **OLIVE OIL**
½ cup (70g) **SUNFLOWER SEEDS**
½ cup (85g) **PUMPKIN SEEDS**
¼ cup (30g) **SESAME SEEDS**
½ tsp **SALT**
3 cups (300g) **GREEN CABBAGE**, finely shredded
1 cup (40g) **KALE**, finely sliced
2 cups (120g) **SILVERBEET** or **SPINACH**, stems removed, finely sliced

GARLIC TAHINI YOGHURT DRESSING
2 cloves **GARLIC**, peeled, finely chopped
ZEST and **JUICE** of ½ a **LEMON**
2½ tbsp **TAHINI**
4 tbsp **PARSLEY**, finely chopped
½ cup (125ml) **NATURAL YOGHURT**
½ tsp **SALT**
Freshly **GROUND BLACK PEPPER**

Trim all the roots off the celeriac and cut off any tough bits. Peel and grate the celeriac. In a small bowl mix the grated celeriac with the lemon water, — this will prevent it from browning.

Place a frying pan over a low heat. Add the olive oil, seeds and salt. Stirring constantly, cook for 1 — 2 minutes, until the seeds are nicely toasted. Remove from the heat and set aside to cool.

To prepare the dressing: in a small bowl mix all the ingredients together.

To serve: drain the lemon water from the celeriac. Place all the ingredients for the salad into a large serving bowl.

Add the toasted seeds and pour over the dressing, then mix until well combined. Season to taste.

Green Goodness Puree

Serves 4 to 6

VEGETARIAN, GF OPTION

A great way of serving up a good dose of greens.

2 cups (250ml) **WATER**
2 tsp powdered **VEGETABLE STOCK**
7 cups (420g) **LEAFY GREENS**, we use a mix of **SPINACH** and **SILVERBEET**, stems removed roughly chopped
50g **BUTTER**
1 **ONION**, peeled, finely diced
2 cloves **GARLIC**, peeled, crushed, finely chopped
2 tbsp **PLAIN FLOUR** or **GLUTEN FREE FLOUR**
½ cup (125ml) **MILK**
½ tsp **SALT** and freshly **GROUND BLACK PEPPER**
¼ cup (20g) **PARMESAN CHEESE** or **TASTY CHEESE**, grated

In a large saucepan add the water and vegetable stock, place over a high heat and bring to the boil. Add the greens and cover with a tight fitting lid.

Cook for a few minutes, until the greens have wilted. Remove from the heat. Drain the greens through a colander, reserving ¼ cup of the cooking liquid.

Place the saucepan back on the heat. Add the butter, onion and garlic. Cook until the onion is translucent and lightly caramelised.

Reduce the heat to low, add the flour, and cook for a few seconds, stirring constantly.

Slowly pour in the milk and reserved cooking liquid while stirring constantly to make a smooth roux. Stir in the salt, pepper and cheese.

Remove from the heat and stir through the greens. Blend into a very smooth puree using a stick blender. Serve with the *PAPER BAKED FISH (see pg 40)* or *PERUVIAN ROAST CHICKEN (see pg 146)*.

Greens w/ Thai Peanut Sauce

Serves 4

VEGAN, GF, DF

THAI PEANUT DRESSING
1 tsp **FRESH GINGER**, grated
1 clove **GARLIC**, peeled, crushed and very finely chopped
1 — 2 tsp **FRESH LIME** or **LEMON JUICE**
1 tbsp **GLUTEN FREE TAMARI SOY SAUCE**
1 tbsp **RICE WINE VINEGAR**
1 tbsp **COCONUT SUGAR** or soft **BROWN SUGAR**
1 — 2 tsp **SRIRACHA** or **CHILLI PASTE** (more if you like it hot)
2 tbsp good quality **CRUNCHY PEANUT BUTTER**
3 tbsp **SALTED ROASTED PEANUTS**, roughly chopped
2 tbsp **PEANUT OIL** or **SESAME OIL**

GREENS
2 tbsp **PEANUT OIL** or **SESAME OIL**
350g **BROCCOLINI** or **BROCCOLI FLORETS**, sliced lengthways into thin strips
300g **SPINACH, KALE** or **CAVOLO NERO**, tough stems removed
600g **ASIAN GREENS (CHOY SUM, PAK CHOY, BOK CHOY, TATSOI)**, roughly chopped

To prepare the dressing: place all the ingredients in a small bowl. Using a fork whisk together until well combined.

Note: this is a traditional Thai style peanut dressing, if you prefer a creamy peanut dressing add ¼ of a cup of coconut cream.

To prepare the greens: place a wok over a high heat and add the oil. When hot, add the broccolini or broccoli and all the greens.

Fry for a few minutes, stirring constantly. Add the peanut dressing and fry for a further minute. Transfer to a serving bowl. Season to taste with salt and freshly ground black pepper.

Turmeric, Lime + Coconut Cauliflower Rice

Serves 4 to 6

VEGAN, GF, DF

Cauliflower rice is a delicious and nutritious alternative to white rice. Serve it with your favourite curry or just eat it by the bowl full as is.

1 large **CAULIFLOWER**, roughly chopped
¼ cup (10g) **FRESH CORIANDER**,
  roughly chopped
1 cup (60g) **SPINACH**, roughly chopped
2 tbsp **COCONUT OIL**
1 tsp **FRESH TURMERIC**, grated or
  ½ tsp **TURMERIC POWDER**
1 **ONION**, peeled, finely diced
3 cloves **GARLIC**, peeled, finely chopped
3 tbsp **DESICCATED COCONUT**

LIME MARINADE
2 tbsp **VEGETABLE OIL**
ZEST and **JUICE** of 1 **LIME**
1 tsp soft **BROWN SUGAR**
1 tsp **CUMIN SEEDS**
1 tsp **SALT**

Place the cauliflower, coriander and spinach in a food processor. Pulse until the cauliflower becomes a fine rice texture. If you don't have a food processor you can use a grater to grate the cauliflower and finely chop the coriander and spinach.

To prepare the marinade: place all the ingredients in a small bowl and whisk together.

To cook the cauliflower ride: place a large frying pan or wok over a medium heat. Add the coconut oil, turmeric, onion and garlic and cook for a few minutes. Add the desiccated coconut and cauliflower rice mixture. Continue to cook for 10 minutes, stirring often.

Pour the marinade over the cauliflower rice. Mix until well combined and cook for a few minutes longer. Remove from the heat and serve.

Dreamy Creamy Cauliflower Puree

Serves 4 to 6

VEGETARIAN, GF

We love pureed cauliflower, it's so delicious. Even if you just add loads of butter, salt and pepper and nothing more, it's perfect. This recipe takes it to the next level of creamy yumminess.

1 **CAULIFLOWER**, roughly chopped
2 tsp **VEGETABLE STOCK POWDER**
¼ cup (60ml) **CREAM** or **SOUR CREAM**
80g **BUTTER**
1 tsp **FRESH** or **DRIED OREGANO**
2 tbsp **FRESH ITALIAN PARSLEY**,
  finely chopped
1 tsp **SALT** and freshly
  GROUND BLACK PEPPER

Place the cauliflower into a large saucepan and fill with enough hot water to cover. Add the vegetable stock powder and cover with a lid.

Place over a high heat and bring to the boil. Cook for 15 minutes, until the cauliflower is very soft. Remove from the heat and drain well.

Transfer the cauliflower into a food processor and add all the remaining ingredients. Blend until very smooth and creamy. Adjust seasoning to taste. Serve as a substitute for mashed potato.

Roasted Persian Cauliflower Steaks

Serves 4

VEGETARIAN, GF, VEGAN OPTION

1 large **CAULIFLOWER**
1 tbsp **SUMAC**
50g **BUTTER**, diced
1 tbsp **POMEGRANATE MOLASSES**

MARINADE
¼ cup (60ml) **OLIVE OIL**
1½ tsp **CUMIN POWDER** or **SEEDS**
ZEST of 1 **LEMON** + 1 tbsp **LEMON JUICE**
2 tsp **HONEY**
1 tbsp **FRESH OREGANO**, finely chopped
2 cloves **GARLIC**, peeled and finely chopped
1 tsp **SALT** and freshly
  GROUND BLACK PEPPER

Preheat oven to 200°C.

Grease and line a baking tray with baking paper.

To prepare the cauliflower: fill a large saucepan with hot water. Place over a high heat and bring to the boil. Once boiling add the whole cauliflower and cook for 10 minutes. Remove from the heat, refresh under cold running water and drain well.

Slice the cauliflower into 1½ cm thick steaks (how many you get will depend on how big the cauliflower is). Transfer the cauliflower steaks and any small florets of cauliflower onto the prepared baking tray.

To prepare the marinade: in a small bowl combine all the ingredients. Brush the marinade onto the cauliflower steaks. Sprinkle the sumac over the cauliflower and add the diced butter to the tray.

Place on the highest shelf in the oven and cook the cauliflower for 25 – 30 minutes or until it is nice and crispy around the edges and cooked through. Drizzle over the pomegranate molasses and serve with *TAHINI SAUCE* (see pg 244) or *CUMIN YOGHURT DIP* (see pg 244).

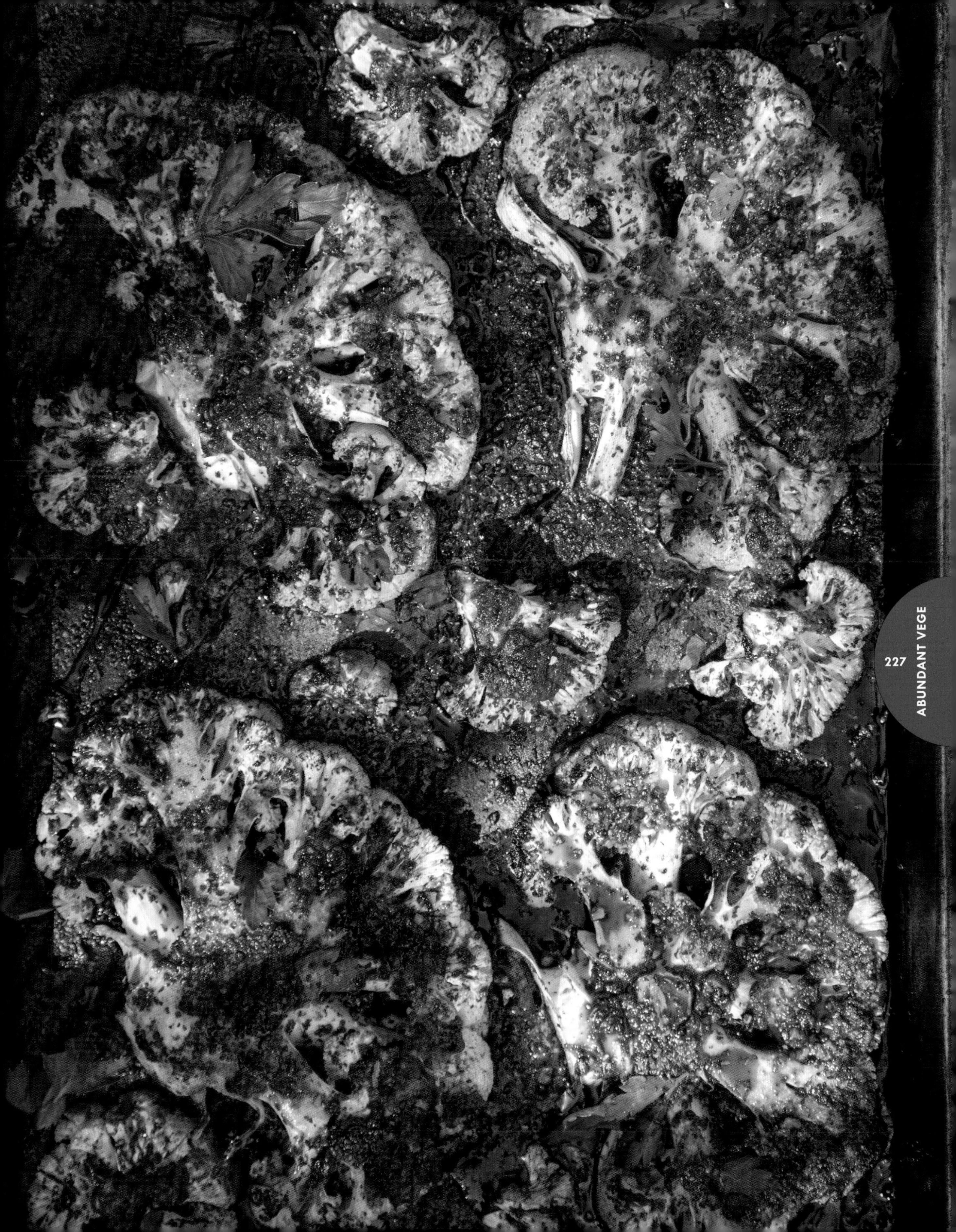

Miso Glazed Butternut

Serves 4

VEGETARIAN, DF

This miso glaze is also yummy on roasted eggplant, tofu, prawns or salmon. It is a great easy glaze to have in the refrigerator for a quick and delicious dinner.

4 tbsp **MISO PASTE**
3 tbsp **VEGETABLE OIL**
2 tbsp **MIRIN**
1 tbsp **SOY SAUCE**
3 – 4 tsp **SAMBAL OELEK** or **SRIRACHA**
1½ tbsp soft **BROWN SUGAR** or **HONEY**
½ large **BUTTERNUT**, skin on, seeds removed, sliced lengthways into wedges
SALT and freshly **GROUND BLACK PEPPER**

Preheat oven to 180°C.

Line a large baking tray with baking paper.

To prepare the miso glaze: in a small bowl mix the miso, oil, mirin, soy sauce, sambal oelek and sugar until well combined.

Place the butternut onto the prepared tray. Drizzle the miso glaze over the butternut and turn to coat in the glaze. Place in the oven to roast for 30 – 35 minutes, or until cooked through and caramelised.

Remove from the oven and transfer onto a serving platter. Season to taste with salt and freshly ground black pepper.

Mexican Pumpkin, Corn + Mozzarella Fritters

Makes 25 fritters.

VEGETARIAN, GF

Everyone loves a good fritter oozing with mozzarella and deep-fried deliciousness. When the winter blues have hit and dinner feels like an irritation this recipe is the perfect escape route. Super easy, super quick and delicious. If you don't have pumpkin, try using kumara, carrot or courgette – they all taste great.

2½ cups (350g) **PUMPKIN**, peeled, grated
1 x 400g can **CORN KERNELS**, drained
1 **RED ONION**, peeled, finely diced
1 cup (100g) **MOZZARELLA CHEESE** or **PIZZA CHEESE**, grated
1 cup (150g) **SELF-RAISING GLUTEN FREE FLOUR**
1 tsp **BAKING POWDER**
1½ tsp **SALT**
2 tsp **MEXICAN** or **CREOLE SPICE MIX**
½ cup (20g) **FRESH CORIANDER** or **PARSLEY**, finely chopped
2 **EGGS**
1 cup (250ml) **MILK**
VEGETABLE OIL for deep-frying

In a large mixing bowl mix all of the ingredients together until well combined.

Place a large saucepan or wok over a medium heat. Add enough oil for deep- frying (approximately 3 cups).

Drop heaped dessertspoon sized spoonfuls of the mixture into the hot oil. Cook a few at a time; don't over crowd the pan, as this will make the fritters hard to turn.

Cook the fritters for a few minutes on each side or until cooked through. Drain well on paper towels. Serve with the *CHIPOTLE MAYO (see pg 146)*.

Roasted Pumpkin w/ Walnut and Feta

Serves 4 to 6

VEGETARIAN, GF

A nice and easy roasted side dish, or add some baby spinach and serve as a salad.

1.5kg **PUMPKIN**, skin on, seeds removed, sliced into wedges
2 **RED ONIONS**, peeled, cut into chunky wedges
3 tbsp **OLIVE OIL**
1 tbsp **HONEY**
½ tsp **FENNEL SEEDS**
½ tsp **SALT**
¼ cup (40g) **PUMPKIN SEEDS**
¼ cup (30g) **WALNUTS**
100g **FETA**

Preheat oven to 180°C.

Line a large roasting tray with baking paper.

In a large mixing bowl combine the pumpkin, onions, olive oil, honey, fennel seeds and salt. Mix until well coated in the oil.

Transfer onto the prepared tray and place in the oven to roast for 20 minutes.

Add the pumpkin seeds and walnuts to the roasting tray, crumble over the feta and cook for 10 minutes longer or until the nuts are toasted.

Fabulous glazes, marinades, sauces and rubs to serve with chicken, fish, seafood, Tofu or Tempeh, for a quick easy meal on those days when you need a little inspiration.

—Rescue Remedies

Ripe's tips on marinating and cooking your favourite protein

At Ripe Deli we serve up trays and trays of marinated chicken breasts and salmon fillets every day. If you are a regular at Ripe you will know how popular these are. We thought it would be a good idea to make a section in the book dedicated to this.

Here is an easy guide to cooking these marinades, on your choice of protein, for a quick and easy meal.

Keep a few of these marinades in the refrigerator ready for those busy meal times when the thought of cooking is daunting, or you just don't know what to cook. Cooking methods are included for chicken, salmon, fish fillets or prawns, as well as tofu and tempeh.

Marinated Salmon or Fish Fillets

Serves 4

*500g – 600g x **FRESH SALMON FILLET**, skin on, bone out, sliced into 4 portions*
*Or 500g – 600g x **FRESH FISH FILLETS**, firm white flesh is best*

To prepare the salmon or fish fillets: preheat oven to 180°C.

Line a baking dish with baking paper. Place ¼ cup of marinade in a mixing bowl, add the salmon or fish fillets and turn to coat. Leave to marinate for at least 10 minutes.

Place the salmon or fish fillets on the prepared baking tray. Bake the salmon fillets for 10 – 12 minutes. Bake fish fillets for 6 – 8 minutes (depends on the size of your fillets) or until just cooked through.

Note: it is better to slightly undercook the fillets as they will continue cooking when removed from the oven.

Marinated Prawns

Serves 4

*600g **FRESH PRAWNS***
*Or defrosted **FROZEN PRAWNS**, de-shelled, tail on*

To prepare the prawns: place ¼ cup of marinade in a mixing bowl, add the prawns and turn to coat. Leave to marinate for at least 10 minutes.

Place a frying pan over a high heat. Add a splash of vegetable oil. When hot add the prawns, along with any marinade left in the bottom of the bowl, to the pan. Fry for a few minutes on each side.

Marinated Tofu or Tempeh

Serves 4

*500g – 600g of **FIRM TOFU** or **TEMPEH** cut into 3cm cubes.*

To prepare the tofu or tempeh: place ¼ cup of marinade in a mixing bowl, add the tofu or tempeh and turn to coat. Leave to marinate for at least 10 minutes.

Place a frying pan over a high heat. Add a splash of vegetable oil. When hot add the tofu or tempeh, along with any marinade that is left in the bottom of the bowl, to the pan. Stir-fry for a few minutes on each side.

Marinated Chicken

Serves 4

*4 x **CHICKEN BREASTS**, skin on, bone out*

To prepare the chicken breasts: preheat oven to 180°C.

Line a roasting dish with baking paper. Place ¼ cup of marinade in a mixing bowl, add the chicken and turn to coat. Leave to marinate for at least 10 minutes.

Sear the chicken breasts by placing a frying pan over a high heat and adding a splash of vegetable oil.

When the oil is hot place the chicken breasts skin side down into the pan. Cook for a few minutes until the skin is browned.

Remove from the heat and place the chicken breasts in the roasting dish. Bake in the oven for 20 – 30 minutes.

Note: smaller breasts will cook quicker — check by slicing through the middle of the largest chicken breast to see if it is cooked all the way through, and that the juices run clear.

Ripe's Rescue Remedies

Marinades, Glazes + Rubs

Tandoori Spice Rub

Makes 1½ cups

GF, DF, VEGAN

Goes well with chicken, salmon, fish, prawns or tofu.

Fragrant Indian spices to delight your senses.

For a delicious traditional Indian tandoori flavour, mix ¼ cup of the marinade with ½ cup of yoghurt and marinate chicken, salmon, or fish pieces in the mix overnight. Thread the marinated pieces onto skewers and grill on the barbeque.

4 tbsp **CORIANDER SEEDS**, *toasted*
4 tbsp **CUMIN SEEDS**, *toasted*
3 **CARDAMOM PODS**, *seeds only*
1 tsp whole **BLACK PEPPERCORNS**
2 tsp **PAPRIKA**
2 tsp **GROUND CINNAMON**
2 tsp **GROUND GINGER**
½ tsp **CHILLI POWDER**
  (optional, add more if you like it spicy)
1 tsp **GROUND TURMERIC**
1 tsp **SALT**
½ cup (125ml) **VEGETABLE OIL**

Place all the ingredients, except the oil, into a spice grinder or food processor and blend well for a few minutes or until all the spices are ground and well combined. Transfer into a clean jar and stir through the oil. This spice mix keeps well in the refrigerator for 6 months.

Balsamic + Fennel Glaze

Makes ½ cup

GF, DF, VEGETARIAN

Goes well with chicken and salmon.

A classic French style glaze that is so easy to whip up.

¼ cup (60ml) **BALSAMIC VINEGAR**
2 tbsp **DRY WHITE WINE**
2 – 3 tbsp **MAPLE SYRUP** or **HONEY**
1 tbsp **DIJON MUSTARD**
1 tsp **FENNEL SEEDS**
1 clove **GARLIC**, *peeled, finely chopped*

Combine all the ingredients for the glaze in a small pot over a low heat and simmer for a few minutes. Remove from the heat and allow to cool. Store in a clean jar in the refrigerator. This marinade keeps well for 2 months in the refrigerator.

Greek Lemon + Herb Marinade

Makes 1 cup

VEGETARIAN, DF, GF

Goes well with chicken, salmon, fish or prawns. Perfect in the summer months with a nice light leafy salad.

ZEST and **JUICE** of 2 **LEMONS**
6 cloves **GARLIC**, *peeled, finely chopped*
2 tbsp **FRESH THYME**, *finely chopped*
1 tbsp **FRESH OREGANO**, *finely chopped*
1 tbsp **WHOLEGRAIN MUSTARD**
1 tsp **SALT**
2 – 3 tbsp **HONEY** or **MAPLE SYRUP**
3 tbsp **OLIVE OIL**
1 whole **LEMON**, *thinly sliced*

In a mixing bowl, mix all the ingredients together. Store in a clean jar in the refrigerator. This marinade keeps well for 2 weeks in the refrigerator.

Buttery Herb, Lemon + Garlic Marinade

Makes ½ cup

GF, VEGETARIAN

Goes well with chicken, salmon, fish or prawns.

A delicious herby marinade that is so quick and easy. Serve with boiled new potatoes and blanched greens for a simple fast meal. You can use any herbs you have growing in the garden at the time.

60g **BUTTER**
2 tbsp **OLIVE OIL**
4 cloves **GARLIC**, *peeled, finely chopped*
2 tbsp **FRESH THYME** *leaves picked*
A handful of **MIXED FRESH HERBS**,
  we used **CHIVES, BASIL** *and* **PARSLEY**,
  finely chopped
2 – 3 tsp **HONEY**
ZEST and **JUICE** of 2 **LEMONS**
SALT and freshly **GROUND BLACK PEPPER**

In a small saucepan over a low heat, melt the butter, olive oil, garlic and thyme together.

Remove from the heat and stir through the mixed herbs, honey, lemon zest and juice.

Season to taste with salt and pepper. Store in a clean jar in the refrigerator. This marinade keeps well for 1 week in the refrigerator.

Balinese Rub

Makes 2 cups

DF, OPTION FOR GF, VEGAN
OR VEGETARIAN

Goes well with chicken, salmon, fish, prawns, tofu and tempeh.

Try this marinade on prawns, fish, beef, pork or chicken cooked on the barbeque, or fried with tofu or tempeh with some coconut cream added to the pan as a divine curry.

Look for Sambal Oelek that contains shrimp, anchovy or fish sauce if you can – this will take this marinade to the next level! For vegans and vegetarians look for one without fish products or see the substitutions in the recipe below. To make this marinade gluten free, use gluten free soy sauce and add an extra tablespoon of honey.

¼ cup (35g) **CASHEW NUTS**, toasted
4 tsp **CORIANDER SEEDS**, toasted
1 tsp **TURMERIC POWDER**
6 **KAFFIR LIME LEAVES**, torn
5 tbsp **SAMBAL OELEK**
  (or use **SRIRACHA** or **CHILLI SAUCE**)
3 small **SHALLOTS** or 1 **RED ONION**,
  peeled, roughly chopped
6 cloves **GARLIC**, peeled, roughly chopped
¼ cup **SESAME OIL**
2 tbsp **COCONUT SUGAR** or soft
  BROWN SUGAR
3 tbsp **KECAP MANIS** (sweet soy sauce)
3 tsp **SALT**
ZEST and **JUICE** of 1 **LIME**

Using a food processor, blend the cashew nuts and coriander seeds for a few minutes, or until they are well ground. Add all the remaining ingredients for the marinade and blend for 3 minutes, until it turns in to a paste.

Store in a clean jar, topped with a little oil. This marinade keeps well in the refrigerator for 2 months.

Red Harissa + Yoghurt Marinade

Makes 1 cup

GF, VEGETARIAN

Goes well with chicken, salmon, fish or prawns.

Transport your senses to the medinas of Morocco with this lovely marinade which has a delicate kick of spice.

½ cup (125ml) **NATURAL YOGHURT**
½ cup (125ml) **RED HARISSA** (see pg 249)
1 tbsp **CUMIN SEEDS**
½ tsp **SALT** and freshly
  GROUND BLACK PEPPER

In a small mixing bowl combine all the ingredients. Store in a clean jar in the refrigerator. This marinade keeps well for a couple of days in the refrigerator. You will find yourself wanting to add it to everything as it is so tasty.

Teriyaki Marinade

Makes 1½ cups

GF, DF, VEGAN

Goes well with chicken, salmon, fish, prawns, tofu or tempeh.

A great quick marinade – smother it over just about any type of protein. Serve with buckwheat noodles and piles of steamed edamame beans.

2 tsp **CORNFLOUR**
¾ cup (180ml) **WATER**
½ cup (125ml) **GLUTEN FREE SOY SAUCE**
¼ cup (40g) soft **BROWN SUGAR**
2 tsp **FRESH GINGER**, peeled, grated
2 cloves **GARLIC**, finely chopped
2 tsp **SESAME OIL**
3 tbsp **MIRIN**

In a small saucepan mix the cornflour with the water Add the remaining ingredients and stir to combine. Place over a medium heat and bring to the boil.

Reduce the heat and simmer for a few minutes or until the sauce has thickened a little. Remove from the heat and allow to cool. This marinade keeps well in the refrigerator for 6 months.

Asian Sticky Barbeque Marinade

Makes 1 cup

GF, DF, VEGAN

Goes well with chicken, salmon, fish, prawns, tofu or tempeh.

A great versatile marinade and it is also delicious as a sauce. Try it as a sauce with panko coated chicken or pork. Stir-fry with tempeh and loads of steamed broccolini.

6 tbsp **GLUTEN FREE SOY SAUCE**
1 tbsp **FRESH LEMON JUICE**
2 tbsp **SRIRACHA CHILLI SAUCE**
2 tbsp **MIRIN**
1 tbsp **SESAME OIL**
2 tbsp soft **BROWN SUGAR**
2 **SPRING ONIONS**, white and green parts,
  finely chopped
2 tsp **GINGER**, peeled and grated
2 cloves **GARLIC**, peeled, finely chopped
1 tbsp **SESAME SEEDS**

Place all the ingredients in a saucepan. Place over a medium heat, bring to a gentle simmer and cook for 5 minutes. Remove from the heat and allow to cool.

Store in a clean jar in the refrigerator. This marinade keeps well in the refrigerator for 2 months.

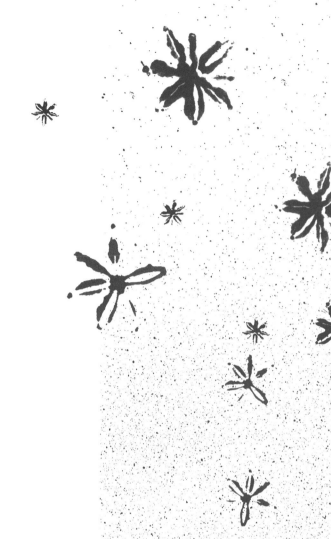

Ripe's special spice mixes and pastes that will tantalise your taste buds.

—Secret Stash

Vegan Laksa Paste

Makes 2 cups

VEGAN, DF, GF

This laksa paste is loaded with flavour with a mild to medium spice level. If you prefer your laksa hotter just add more dried chillies or add some fresh ones as well! Look for the long thin red Asian dried chillies for this recipe. Be careful not to buy the little dried bullet or Birdseye chillies as they are not for the faint hearted and will blow your mind if you are not a chilli lover.

15 – 20 **DRIED RED CHILLIES**

½ cup (70g) **ROASTED CASHEW NUTS**, roughly chopped

5 – 6 (200g) **SHALLOTS**, peeled, roughly chopped

8 cloves **GARLIC**, peeled, roughly chopped

3 tbsp **LEMONGRASS PASTE** or 4 **STEMS** of **LEMONGRASS**, white part finely sliced

10 **KAFFIR LIME LEAVES**, roughly chopped

4cm piece **FRESH GINGER** or **GALANGAL**, grated

1 tbsp **TURMERIC POWDER** or grated **FRESH TURMERIC**

1 tbsp **GROUND CUMIN**

2 tbsp **CORIANDER SEEDS**

1 tbsp **PAPRIKA**

½ cup (20g) **FRESH CORIANDER**, roots, stems and leaves roughly chopped

2½ tsp **SALT**

2 tbsp **COCONUT SUGAR**

3 tbsp **SRIRACHA** or **CHILLI PASTE**

¼ cup **VEGETABLE OIL** or **COCONUT OIL** + 3 tbsp extra for frying

Place the dried chillies into a small bowl and cover with freshly boiled hot water. Soak for 10 minutes, then drain well.

Using a food processor, blend the chillies with the cashew nuts and shallots into a paste. Add the remaining ingredients and blend together for a few minutes until they form a well-combined paste.

Place a large frying pan over a low heat and add the extra 3 tablespoons of oil. When hot, add the paste and fry for 10 minutes stirring constantly. When you can see the oil is starting to separate from the paste it is ready.

Store in a clean jar, topped with a little oil, in the refrigerator for up to 3 months.

We use this laksa paste in our *VEGAN LAKSA* on *pg 188.*

Persian Spice Mix

Makes 1 cup

VEGAN, GF, DF

It's far superior to use whole spices and freshly grind them, as the flavour is incredible. If you don't have any way of grinding them you can use the pre-ground spices, but you will have to grind star anise somehow – try smashing it up using a rolling pin, a rock or a hammer!

You can add this spice mix to slow cooked stews; it's lovely in pumpkin soup. Cook it with tomatoes, eggplant, courgette and French lentils as a middle eastern version of ratatouille. The options are endless but one thing is certain, as soon as you start grinding this spice mix you'll want to cook something with it.

2 tbsp **WHOLE BLACK PEPPERCORNS** (or 1 tbsp of **GROUND BLACK PEPPER**)

3 tbsp **CORIANDER SEEDS** (or 2 tbsp of **GROUND CORIANDER**)

2 tbsp **CUMIN SEEDS** (or 1½ tbsp of **GROUND CUMIN**)

2 tbsp **FENNEL SEEDS** (or 1½ tbsp of **GROUND FENNEL**)

1½ tbsp **WHOLE ALLSPICE BERRIES** (or 1 tbsp of **GROUND ALLSPICE**)

1½ tbsp **CARDAMOM SEEDS** or 80 **PODS**, seeds only (or 1 tbsp of **GROUND CARDAMOM**)

4 **WHOLE CLOVES** (or ½ tsp of **GROUND CLOVES**)

2 x **CINNAMON QUILLS**, approximately 4cm long (or 2 tbsp of **GROUND CINNAMON**)

5 **WHOLE STAR ANISE**

2 tbsp **SMOKED PAPRIKA**

3 tsp **SALT**

Grind all the spices together in a spice grinder, coffee grinder, or use your muscles and pound the spices in a mortar and pestle — a great job to give to kids! Store in a clean jar with a tight fitting lid in the cupboard for up to 2 months.

This spice mix is delicious rubbed on meats, poultry and fish, or sprinkled over vegetables when roasting them.

Serve it sprinkled over hummus or yoghurt. Add 1 tablespoon to ¼ cup of extra virgin olive oil as a dip for warm Turkish bread.

Use this spice mix for our *PERSIAN SLOW ROASTED LAMB* (see pg 150) and in the *PORTOBELLO MUSHROOMS TOPPED WITH PERSIAN LENTILS* (see pg 120).

Japanese Seaweed Sprinkle – Furikake

Makes approximately 1 cup

GF, DF, VEGAN

This little sprinkle will make your taste buds sing, and gives a delicious Japanese flavour to everything you sprinkle it on! Try it straight on avocado or on sushi rice.

3 sheets **NORI**, toasted
½ cup (60g) **SESAME SEEDS**, toasted
2 tsp **FLAKY SEA SALT**
1 tsp **RAW SUGAR**
1 – 2 tsp **CHILLI FLAKES**
2 tsp **CRISPY FRIED SHALLOTS**

To prepare the nori: using tongs, lightly toast it over a gas flame, or if you don't have gas you can toast them in a frying pan or in the oven — the nori will change colour slightly and become crispy. It only takes a few minutes.

To prepare the furikake: break up the nori sheets with your hands and place in a food processor. Add the toasted sesame seeds, salt, sugar, chilli flakes and crispy shallots. Blend for a few minutes until well combined.

Store in a clean jar with a tight fitting lid in the cupboard for up to a month. We use this sprinkled on our *HAWAIIAN POKE SALAD BOWLS (see pg 64)* and the *YUM YUM SUSHI SALAD (see pg 130).*

Dukkah

Makes 3 cups

GF, DF, VEGAN

We love dukkah. It's great sprinkled on just about anything savoury, and especially delish on smashed avocado. Add a couple of tablespoons to some olive oil as a moreish dip or sprinkle it over hummus. It's great to have a secret stash on hand to add to your salads and meals to make them pop with flavour. Dukkah also makes a pretty lovely gift.

¾ cup (90g) **SESAME SEEDS**
5 tbsp (20g) **CORIANDER SEEDS**
3 tbsp (20g) **CUMIN SEEDS**
2 tbsp (10g) **FENNEL SEEDS**
2 cups (240g) **NATURAL ROASTED ALMONDS**
1 tsp **TURMERIC POWDER**
½ tsp **WHOLE BLACK PEPPERCORNS**
2 tsp **SALT**

Place a large frying pan over a medium heat. Add the sesame, coriander, cumin and fennel seeds. Lightly toast the seeds until they are aromatic, stirring constantly so they don't burn.

Using a food processor, lightly blend the almonds until they are roughly broken up. Add the toasted seeds, turmeric, peppercorns and salt. Blend well for a few minutes until the almonds and seeds are ground up.

Dukkah will last for a few months stored in clean sealed jars in the pantry or cupboard.

You will find this used in our *MOROCCAN CARROT SALAD* (see pg 136) and *HARISSA SPICED CARROT PUREE* (see pg 222). At Ripe we often serve boiled eggs rolled in dukkah as tasty protein boost for our salads. We also coat whole salmon fillets in labneh and sprinkle generous amounts of dukkah over the top before baking it.

Condiments that compliment! Dips, sauces, mayo's, pickles, chutneys, and relishes to add the wow factor to your meal.

—A Bit on the Side

A BIT ON THE SIDE

Cumin Yoghurt Dip

Makes 1 cup

GF

So simple but oh so tasty!

1 cup (250ml) **NATURAL YOGHURT**
1 clove **GARLIC**, peeled, finely chopped
2 tsp **CUMIN SEEDS**, toasted
1 tbsp **LEMON JUICE**
½ tsp **SALT**

In a small serving bowl combine all the ingredients. Set aside for 5 minutes to allow the flavours to infuse.

Serve with toasted pita and *DUKKAH (see pg 241)*. Pour it over roasted vegetables, use instead of mayonnaise in a slaw, or dip raw broccoli in it as a snack. We serve this on the *KEDGEREE WITH SMOKED FISH (see pg 190)* and with *AMY'S DHAL FRY (see pg 172)*.

Okonomiyaki Sauce – A Japanese Barbeque Sauce + Marinade

Makes 1 cup

GF OPTION, DF

Use this sauce to marinate meat, prawns or tofu to grill on the barbeque. Try adding a couple of tablespoons to noodles and chicken when making a stir-fry. This sauce is used on our Okonomiyaki Pancake (see pg 14).

½ cup (125ml) good quality **GLUTEN FREE TOMATO SAUCE**
3 tbsp **WORCESTERSHIRE SAUCE**
  (see note below for gluten free option)
1 tsp **DIJON MUSTARD**
4 tbsp of **SAKE** or **RICE WINE**
2 tbsp **GLUTEN FREE SOY SAUCE**
3 tbsp soft **BROWN SUGAR** or **HONEY**
1 tbsp **FRESH GINGER**, grated

Place all the ingredients in a small saucepan over a medium heat and bring to the boil. Reduce the heat and cook for 5 minutes until thickened.

Remove from the heat and set aside to cool. Stored in a sterile jar, this sauce will keep well for a few months in the refrigerator.

Note: a lot of Worcestershire sauce brands contain gluten. To make this gluten free we used Whitlock's Worcestershire sauce. Most good quality tomato sauces and ketchups are gluten free, but again, some are not so check the label!

Tahini Sauce

Makes approximately 1 cup

VEGAN, GF, DF

A fantastic Middle Eastern sauce loaded with goodness and flavour. Drizzle it over falafels or lamb kebabs, pour it over smashed avocado on toast, or dip vegetable sticks into it as a snack.

½ cup (100g) **TAHINI**
¼ cup (60ml) **WATER**
¼ cup (60ml) **OLIVE OIL**
2 cloves **GARLIC**, peeled, finely chopped
½ tsp **SALT**
¼ tsp freshly **GROUND BLACK PEPPER**
1 tsp **GROUND CUMIN**
1 tsp **GROUND CORIANDER**
2 tbsp **FRESH LIME** or **LEMON JUICE**

Place all the ingredients into a bowl and whisk together using a fork until smooth and creamy. This sauce stores well in the refrigerator for up to 2 weeks.

Ripe's Japanese Mayos

Makes 2 cups

VEGETARIAN, GF, DF

Japanese mayo is divine, but unfortunately most contain gluten and dashi stock, which contains fish – which is not suitable for a lot of our customers – so we made our own versions and have also included a vegetarian dashi stock recipe!

JAPANESE MAYO
1½ tbsp **GRAPEFRUIT** or **LEMON JUICE** (or **YUZU** if you can find it!)
2 tbsp **CASTER SUGAR**
½ tsp **SALT**
2 tbsp **RICE VINEGAR**
2 tsp **DIJON MUSTARD**
1 tbsp **DASHI STOCK** or **JAPANESE SOUP STOCK** (see pg 245)
½ tsp **GLUTEN FREE SOY SAUCE**
2 large **EGG YOLKS**, at room temperature
1¾ cups (420ml) **RICE BRAN OIL**

In a small bowl mix the grapefruit juice or lemon juice, caster sugar, salt, vinegar, Dijon mustard, dashi and soy sauce together.

Using a food processor, blend the egg yolks for 3 — 4 minutes until they are creamy, warm and light yellow.

With the motor running, slowly pour in the oil a little at a time — you need to do this really slowly so the oil can emulsify into the egg yolks.

Once the mayo is thick, with the motor still running, start alternating between adding some of the oil and some of the vinegar mix until all of it is incorporated.

Store in clean sterilised jars in the refrigerator for up to 2 weeks. We use *JAPANESE MAYO* on our *OKONOMIYAKI PANCAKE (see pg 14).*

JAPANESE SESAME MAYO
1 cup (250ml) **JAPANESE MAYO**
1 tbsp **GLUTEN FREE SOY SAUCE**
2 tbsp **TOASTED SESAME SEEDS**
2 tbsp **DARK TOASTED SESAME OIL**

Place the Japanese mayo into a small bowl or jar. Using a fork mix through the soy sauce, sesame seeds and sesame oil.

Store in a clean sterilised jar in the refrigerator for up to 2 weeks. We use this on our *HAWAIIAN POKE SALAD BOWLS (see pg 64)* and *YUM YUM SUSHI SALAD WITH HOT SMOKED SALMON (see pg 130).*

Seaweed Dashi Stock

VEGAN, GF, DF

Dashi stock is a delicious Japanese stock made from seaweed, bonito flakes and dried tuna – it's found in Asian supermarkets or in the international section of the supermarket.

For a vegan/vegetarian friendly version follow our recipe below for seaweed dashi. You can of course get inventive with this recipe; try adding some fresh ginger and turmeric root for added flavour.

4 pieces (20g) **DRIED KOMBU KELP**, the big flat seaweed
1 cup **DRIED SHITAKE MUSHROOMS**
4 lt **WATER**

Rinse the seaweed under warm running water.

In a large stockpot or saucepan, add the kelp, shitake mushrooms and water. Place over a medium heat and bring to the boil. Once boiling reduce the heat and gently simmer for 30 minutes.

Remove from the heat. Remove the kelp and shitake mushrooms. Strain the stock through a fine sieve; squeeze any liquid out of the shitake mushrooms.

The shitake mushrooms and kelp can be chopped up and added to a rice salad or a miso broth — kelp is also great for the garden!

The dashi stock is now ready to use or will keep for a few weeks in the refrigerator. Dashi also freezes well — try freezing it in ice cube trays, for handy healthy vegan/vegetarian stock cubes.

Crunchy Refrigerator Pickles

Great as a snack, add them to salads, sandwiches or burgers. Use the pickle juice as a dressing for salads.

Pickled Candy Coloured Beets w/ Star Anise

Makes 2 x 1lt jars

VEGAN, GF, DF

2 x 1lt **PRESERVING JARS**
600g **RED BEETROOTS**, *peeled, thinly sliced*
600g **CANDY STRIPED BEETROOT (CHIOGGIA BEETS)**, *peeled, thinly sliced*

PICKLING LIQUID

3 cups (750ml) **APPLE CIDER VINEGAR**
1 cup (250ml) **WATER**
1 cup (225g) **RAW SUGAR** or **COCONUT SUGAR**
2cm piece of **FRESH GINGER**, *thinly sliced*
2 tsp **PICKLING SPICES**
3 – 4 **WHOLE STAR ANISE**

Turmeric Spiced Cauliflower + Carrot Pickles

Makes 2 x 1lt jars

VEGAN, GF, DF

2 x 1lt **PRESERVING JARS**
6 **CARROTS**, *peeled and cut into thin sticks*
½ **CAULIFLOWER**, *sliced into small bite sized florets*

PICKLING LIQUID

3 cups (750ml) **APPLE CIDER VINEGAR**
1 cup (250ml) **WATER**
1 cup (225g) **RAW SUGAR** or **COCONUT SUGAR**
4cm piece **FRESH TURMERIC**, *thinly sliced*
2cm piece **FRESH GINGER**, *thinly sliced*
2 tsp **PICKLING SPICES**
2 tsp **CURRY POWDER**
2 tsp **CUMIN SEEDS**

Sterilise your jars by filling them with freshly boiled hot water then, after a few minutes, carefully tip out the hot water. Soak the lids in hot water as well.

Tightly pack each type of vegetable separately into a sterilised jar.

Place all the ingredients for the pickling liquid into a large saucepan. Place over a high heat and bring to a rolling boil.

Pour the boiling hot pickling liquid and spices over the vegetables. The pickling liquid should completely cover the vegetables.

Note: if you need more liquid you can just heat up a little more cider vinegar and water with some sugar and pour it over the top. Seal the jars with a tight fitting sterile lid. These pickles are ready to eat in a couple of days, if you can wait that long! Store them in the refrigerator.

Turkish Pickles

Makes approximately 2 x 500ml Jars

VEGETARIAN, GF, DF

These moreish pickles are so delicious you will find it hard not to eat them all straight away. We had to guard them so they didn't all disappear before we had a chance to photograph them for the book!

1¼ cup (310ml) **WATER**

1 tbsp **SALT**

5 tbsp **HONEY**

1 tsp **CARAWAY SEEDS**

5 WHOLE BLACK PEPPERCORNS

2 **FRESH BAY LEAVES**

2 cloves **GARLIC**, peeled, lightly smashed

1½ cups (375ml) **CIDER VINEGAR**

2 **BEETROOT**, peeled, cut into matchsticks

4 **TURNIPS** or **SWEDES**, peeled, cut into matchsticks

In a medium sized saucepan, add the water, salt, honey, caraway seeds, peppercorns, bay leaves and garlic. Place over a medium heat and cook for a minute or until the salt and honey are completely dissolved.

Add the vinegar and bring to the boil. When boiling, add the beetroot and turnips. Cook for a few minutes then remove from the heat.

Transfer the beets and turnips into hot sterilised jars. Pour over the hot pickling liquid. Fill the jars to the top, completely covering the vegetables in pickling liquid. Seal with a sterile tight-fitting lid.

Once sealed these pickles will keep for months. Store in the refrigerator once opened.

Serve as a salad by mixing some of the pickles and some of the pickle liquid through shredded red cabbage and rocket. Use as a pickle in sandwiches or with falafels and hummus in a wrap. We serve these pickles with *RIPE'S CORNED BEEF (see pg 196)*.

Indian Green Coconut Chutney

Serves 6 to 8

VEGAN, GF, DF

This fresh and fragrant chutney is a great addition to any Indian meal or as a delicious vegan dip with toasted chapatti.

1 cup (100g) **FRESH COCONUT**, grated or **DESICCATED COCONUT**

½ cup (125ml) **COCONUT CREAM**

1½ cups (60g) **FRESH CORIANDER**, stem and leaves roughly chopped

2 **SPRING ONIONS**, white and green parts, chopped

1 tsp **COCONUT SUGAR**

1 tsp **SALT**

ZEST and JUICE of 1 **LIME** or ½ **LEMON**

2 tbsp **COCONUT OIL** or **VEGETABLE OIL**

½ tsp **BLACK MUSTARD SEEDS**

2 tsp **CUMIN SEEDS**

2 tsp **FRESH GINGER**, grated

1 – 2 **GREEN CHILLIES**, seeds removed if you don't like it hot, finely chopped

1 sprig of **FRESH CURRY LEAVES**

Note: if you are using desiccated coconut soak the coconut in ¼ cup of boiling water for 5 minutes first to soften it.

Using a food processor, blend the freshly grated coconut (or desiccated coconut soaked in water). Add the coconut cream, coriander, spring onions, sugar, salt, lime or lemon zest and juice.

Blend for a few minutes until the coriander has turned the coconut mixture very green. Pour into a serving dish.

Place a small frying pan over a high heat, add the oil, mustard seeds, cumin seeds, ginger, chillies and curry leaves.

Stir-fry for a few minutes until fragrant and the mustard seeds start popping. Remove from the heat, pour over the coconut mixture and serve.

Note: if you would like to make this coconut chutney in advance then just gently heat it slightly before serving, as the coconut oils solidify in the refrigerator.

This chutney keeps well stored in the refrigerator for up to a week.

Fiery African Roasted Tomato Sauce

Makes approximately 2 x 1lt bottles

GF, DF, VEGAN

A wonderfully rich, smoky and sweetly spiced tomato sauce. Any dried red chilli will work but for a complex smoky flavour use a mix of chillies. Ancho Poblano is mild and smoky, Guajillo Chillies or Jalapeno both have a mild to medium heat, or if you love a fire in your belly add some Birds Eye Chillies, which give a good kick of heat.

2 kg **RIPE TOMATOES**, *the riper and juicer the better*
3 **ONIONS**, *peeled, chopped into chunky wedges*
¼ cup (60ml) **OLIVE OIL**
15 **DRIED RED CHILLIES**
1 whole bulb **GARLIC**, *cloves separated, peeled, crushed and roughly chopped*
2 tbsp **GROUND CORIANDER**
2 tbsp **SMOKED PAPRIKA**
2 tbsp **SWEET PAPRIKA**
1 cup (250ml) **RED WINE VINEGAR**
1 cup (220g) **WHITE SUGAR** or **RAW SUGAR**
2 tsp **SALT**
1 tsp freshly **GROUND BLACK PEPPER**

Preheat oven to the highest grill setting.

To prepare the tomatoes and onions: place the tomatoes and onions in a large roasting dish. Pour the olive oil over and turn to coat the tomatoes and onions in the oil.

Place on the highest shelf the oven to roast for 20 – 25 minutes or until the tomatoes are soft and juicy and the skins are charred and smoky.

To prepare the chillies: place the chillies in a bowl and cover with a cup of boiling water. Cover the bowl with a plate and leave to soak for approximately 15 minutes. Drain and discard the water.

To cook the tomato sauce: tip the roasted tomatoes, onions and all of the juices from the roasting tray into a large stockpot or preserving pan. Add the garlic, coriander and paprika.

Place over a medium heat and cook for a few minutes stirring often. Add the chillies, vinegar, sugar, salt, pepper and bring to the boil.

When boiling, reduce the heat to as low as possible and cook for 40 minutes. Remove from the heat then blend well using a stick blender.

Pour into clean, hot sterilised bottles and seal with a clean lid. This tomato sauce will last for months stored in the pantry or cupboard. Once open store in the refrigerator.

The Great Tomato Relish

Makes approximately 5 x 350ml jars

VEGAN, DF

This relish has stood the test of time; it was my grandmother, Helen Rutledge's recipe and has been passed down through the generations.

Use big, fat, juicy, ripe tomatoes and preferably home grown for this recipe, as they will give the best flavour. If you would like to make this recipe gluten free, use cider vinegar instead of malt vinegar.

1 – 2kg **TOMATOES**, *core removed, tomatoes left whole*
1kg **APPLES**, *peeled, core removed and roughly diced*
1kg **ONIONS**, *peeled, roughly diced*
500g **WHITE SUGAR**
2 tbsp **SALT**
3 tsp **MILD CURRY POWDER**
3 tsp **GROUND GINGER**
½ – 1 tsp **CAYENNE PEPPER**
½ tsp **GROUND CLOVES**
3 cups **MALT VINEGAR**

Tip: using a small paring knife cut a small cross on the bottom of each tomato – this will make it much easier to remove the skin once they have been soaked in the boiling water.

To prepare the tomatoes: place the tomatoes into a large bowl and cover them with boiling hot water. Leave to soak for 15 – 20 minutes.

Peel the skin off the tomatoes and roughly chop them into a large stockpot or preserving pan. Add the apples, onions, sugar, salt, all the spices and the malt vinegar.

Place over a medium heat and bring to the boil. Once boiling reduce the heat to as low as possible. Gently simmer for 1 – 1½ hours, stirring the relish every so often.

While the relish is cooking give it a good mash with a potato masher every now and then to make sure the apple is well mashed up, as this is what thickens the relish.

Spoon into hot, clean sterilised jars with clean tight fitting lids. Store in the pantry or cupboard for up to 2 years.

Red Harissa

Makes 3 x 200ml jars

VEGETARIAN, GF, DF, VEGAN OPTION

A divine sweetly spiced Moroccan sauce or marinade. This Harissa is so delicious and adds an amazing burst of flavour to everything you add it to. Try some on poached eggs with avocado, or for an easy dinner rub some of it over a whole chicken before roasting.

8 – 10 **DRIED RED CHILLIES**

1 x 680g jar **ROASTED RED PEPPERS**, drained or 10 **RED CAPSICUMS**, de-seeded, roasted and peeled

4 cloves **GARLIC**, peeled, crushed

2 tbsp **SMOKED PAPRIKA**

2 tbsp **CORIANDER SEEDS**, toasted

2 tbsp **CUMIN SEEDS**, toasted

1½ tbsp **SALT**

2 tbsp soft **BROWN SUGAR** or **HONEY**

¼ cup (60ml) **FRESH LEMON JUICE**

½ cup (125ml) **OLIVE OIL** + extra for the jars

In a small bowl, place the dried chillies and add a cup of freshly boiled hot water. Cover with a plate and leave to soak for 30 minutes.

Drain the chillies and discard the liquid. If you are using fresh capsicums follow the instructions for preparing the capsicums in the **TOMATO AND ROAST CAPSICUM PANZANELLA SALAD (see pg 220).**

Using a food processor, blend the chillies until they are well chopped. Add the remaining ingredients then blend into a fine paste.

Pour the harissa into sterilised jars, top with a little olive oil and seal with a clean tight fitting lid. Store in the refrigerator. We use this in our **ROCK THE CASBAH SALAD (see pg 132), RED HARISSA + YOGHURT MARINADE FOR CHICKEN (see pg 235)** and the **HARISSA SPICED CARROT PUREE (see pg 222).**

Index

Y

Z

259 INDEX

—Thank You

We got the majority of the dream team back together again to make this book "A Third Helping" happen.

Without creative director and project manager Amy Melchior this book would never have gone to print! So a big thank you Amy from the bottom of my heart for the passion, enthusiasm and creative wonder you put into this project and many others at Ripe. You are a true inspiration to me and the team.

We were lucky that Andrea Saunders was available to once again help Amy in the test kitchen. They did an amazing job.

To the fabulous team at Ripe Deli who shared their best creations and whipped up recipes to fill the gaps – you can be proud of what you have done here and contributed to.

To our friends and suppliers who have contributed your fabulous recipes that have made this book a family affair.

Sally Greer at Beatnik Publishing for once again producing and designing a book full of your stunning photography that we are so very proud of.

Lisa Clarke for coming on board to make sure we made as few mistakes as possible.

Emma and Tana at Akin design for our exciting new brand direction.

Al Keating for nailing the title of the book.

Jo Bridgford for a great box of china.

Debbie Harrison at Casual Fridays for having a wicked way with words.

Greg, Sam and Jessica Snelgrove for encouraging me to keep taking risks, backing me all the way and giving me lots of love and support.

A special big thank you to each and every one of you who has purchased and fallen in love with our cookbooks.

Finally to all the Ripe Deli customers for all your support and for being a special part of the Ripe Deli family.

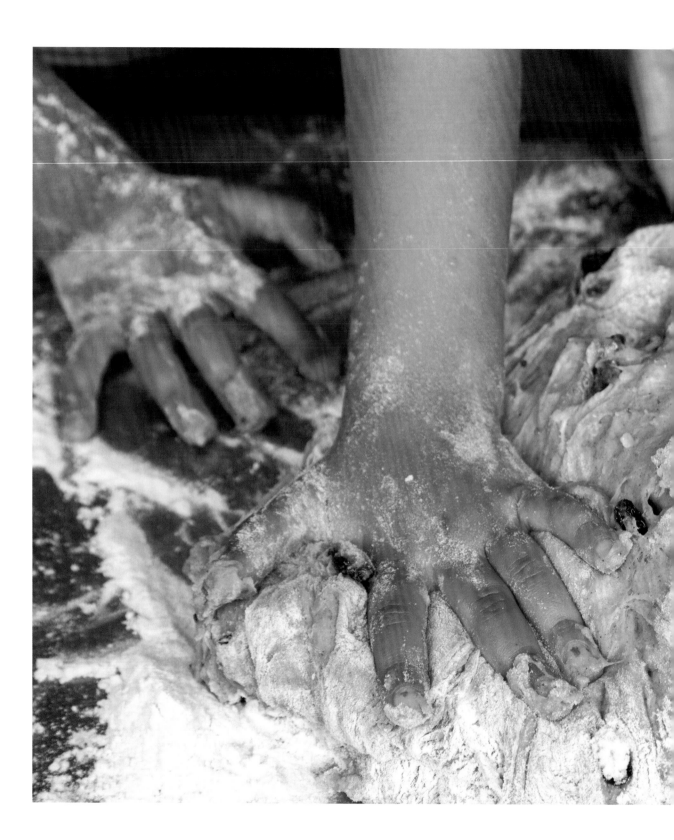

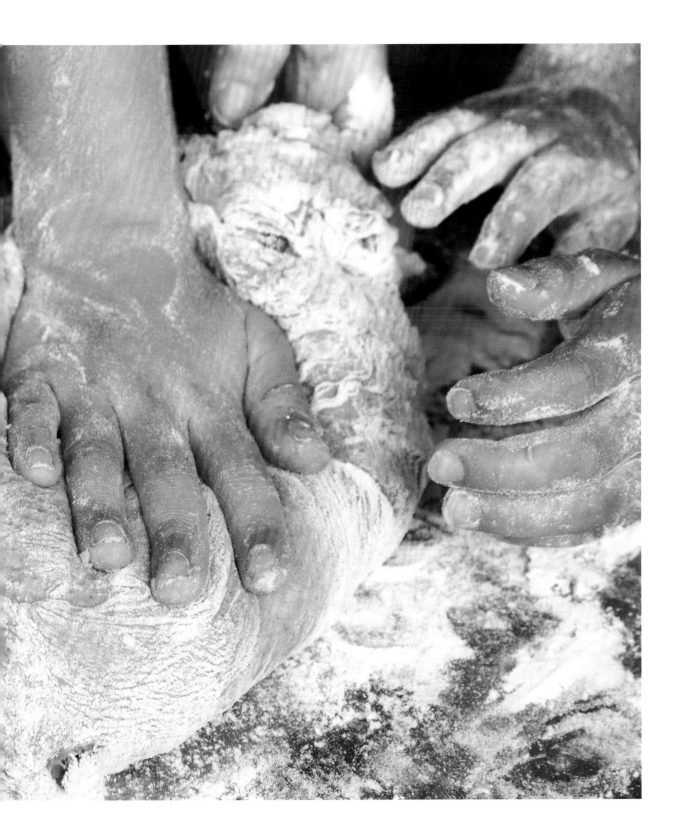

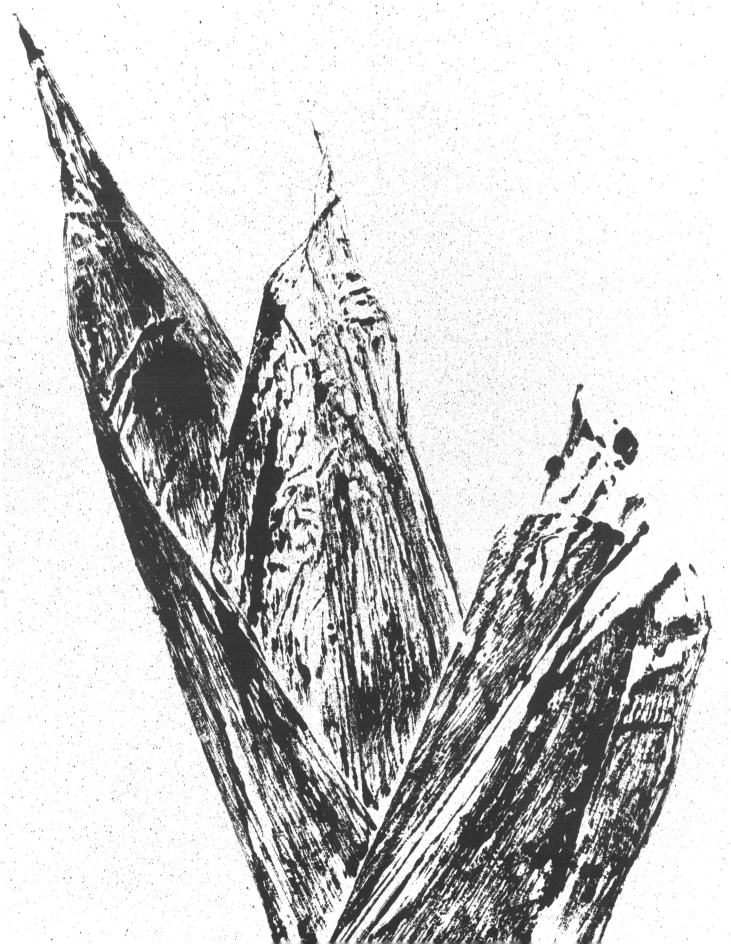